NOSTRADAMUS
AND BEYOND

NOSTRADAMUS AND BEYOND

INCLUDING 128 NEW PROPHECIES BASED ON HIS TECHNIQUES

*"Our chief interest in the past
is as a guide to the future."*

DEAN W. R. INGE:
Assessments and Anticipations

PETER LEMESURIER

A GODSFIELD BOOK

Library of Congress Cataloging-in-Publication Data Available

10 9 8 7 6 5 4 3 2 1

Published in 1999 by Sterling Publishing Company, Inc.
387 Park Avenue South, New York, N.Y. 10016
© 1999 Godsfield Press
Text © 1998 Peter Lemesurier

Peter Lemesurier asserts the moral right to be identified
as the author of this work.

Designed for Godsfield Press by
THE BRIDGEWATER BOOK COMPANY

Distributed in Canada by Sterling Publishing
c/o Canadian Manda Group, One Atlantic Avenue, Suite 105
Toronto, Ontario, Canada M6K 3E7
Distributed in Australia by Capricorn Link (Australia) Pty Ltd
P.O. Box 6651, Baulkham Hills, Business Centre, NSW 2153, Australia

Printed and bound in Hong Kong

ISBN 0-8069-9911-X

Numerals in superscript refer to the Bibliography on page 124.

CONTENTS

INTRODUCTION   6

PART 1
THE SEER AND HIS PROPHECIES   9

NOSTRADAMUS: MAN AND SEER   10

THE METHOD REVEALED   18

EVIDENCE   22

NOSTRADAMUS'S OTHER TECHNIQUES   30

CRACKING THE DATING CODE   38

THE NEW MILLENNIUM   44

PART 2
THE NEW PROPHECIES   55

GUIDE TO THE NEW PROPHECIES   56

PROLOGUE   58

THE NEW PROPHECIES   60

BIBLIOGRAPHY   124

INDEX   126

ACKNOWLEDGMENTS   128

INTRODUCTION

The real facts about the life of Nostradamus have often been inaccurately reported.

UP UNTIL THE EARLY 1990s there were virtually no English-language books on Nostradamus that could be relied upon either for their translations or for their biographical facts. This was nothing new. The unfortunate tradition went right back to the very first book in the genre – namely Garencières's celebrated but deeply flawed edition of 1672. Only James Randi's characteristically skeptical study of 1990 was even remotely up-to-date with its research.

The French were much better provided for. They had their Leroy and Dupèbe, their Amadou and Benazra, their Chomarat and Laroche. The French Canadians, similarly, had their Dufresne and Brind'Amour. All of them had written (or were in the process of writing) superb books on the sixteenth-century seer, all of them founded squarely on detailed academic research into the now freely available archives.

By contrast, most of the available books in English were such crude, amateurish, ill-informed, linguistically inaccurate, credulous, and sometimes tendentious farragoes of nonsense that it was tempting to wonder whether their authors were even competent in French, let alone in Nostradamus's sixteenth-century version of it.

The restored house in Salon-de-Provence where Nostradamus spent much of his later life.

THE FIRST SEQUENCED
ENGLISH VERSE-TRANSLATION

In my *Nostradamus: The Next 50 Years* of 1993, therefore, I attempted to remedy the situation by publishing what I hoped was the first readable and reasonably accurate English translation of over 400 of the seer's *Propheties* – and certainly the first sequenced *verse*-translation of them. In my subsequent *Nostradamus: The Final Reckoning* of 1995 I attempted additionally to provide some kind of dating-framework, along with illustrative maps. The appreciative response from readers of the book – from all around the world – suggested that the initiative was long overdue.

There still remained, however, the wholesale biographical delusions that had by then been published and accepted worldwide as though they were established fact. Apart from the details of the seer's dates of birth and death, scarcely any of the statements in the more popular English-language books about him could be trusted. It was not just that most of them were hopelessly inaccurate. What was more confidence-sapping was the fact that the lay reading public naturally had no means of telling the few that were actually true from those that were inaccurate.

I therefore attempted to rectify this embarrassing situation in my *Nostradamus Encyclopedia* of 1997, in the process taking the recent French research and making a good deal of it available to the English-speaking public for the first time.

THE PRESENT VOLUME

In the present book I have taken the opportunity to enlarge on that information and reveal a few more of the facts that the research has recently turned up. I have traced what is now known to be the real story of Nostradamus's life. I have explained the ways in which his thinking was conditioned by the characteristic cosmological and astrological conceptions of his age. I have reconstructed how he probably hit on his astrological method as a result of the great planetary conjunction of 1524. I have explained in detail the resulting technique of "comparative horoscopy" and illustrated it with previously unpublished charts. I have shown how he used it to predict the recurrence of specific historical events

and how, on this basis, it is nowadays possible for us to date and sequence many of his prophecies. And I have, on this same basis, attempted an outline of our likely destiny over the coming decades, at least as he seems to have foreseen it.

NEW PROPHECIES

Indeed, so clearly does Nostradamus's prophetic methodology emerge from the process that, in Part 2, I have felt confident enough to stick my neck out and apply that methodology for myself.

Not everybody will thank me for this unexpected bonus. But at least it may provide some useful feedback not merely on the validity or non-validity of the technique itself, but on my success or otherwise in applying it.

Whether it also sheds any further light on our likely future, though – or, indeed, on Nostradamus's degree of success in predicting it – only the future itself can possibly tell.

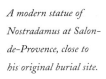

A modern statue of Nostradamus at Salon-de-Provence, close to his original burial site.

PART 1

THE SEER AND HIS PROPHECIES

NOSTRADAMUS: MAN AND SEER

Michel de Nostredame was born in St.-Rémy-de-Provence on December 14th, 1503 to Reynière and Jaume (James) de Nostredame. Jaume was a prosperous merchant of Jewish extraction who, within a few years, would also take on the role of home-grown lawyer. At least one handwritten legal deed of the latter's survives, duly signed with the Latinized form of his name, *Jacobus de nostra domina.*

CHILDHOOD AND EDUCATION

The eldest son of at least eight children, it is possible that Michel was educated initially by his maternal great-grandfather, Jean de St.-Rémy, a doctor and former treasurer of the town. If so, his studies would no doubt have included the classical trivium of grammar, rhetoric, and logic, as well as mathematics, astronomy, chemistry, and a smattering of medicine and herbalism. There is good evidence, too, that (true to the classically minded spirit of his age) the boy was fascinated by the nearby ruins of Glanum, an important former Greco-Roman city that lay just to the south of the town, below the northern foothills of the Alpilles. True, the extensive ruins that can be visited today alongside the former priory of St.-Paul-de-Mausole (latterly an asylum, and now a psychiatric clinic named after its most famous former patient, Vincent van Gogh) had not yet been excavated, but the great town gate stood proud and strong, alongside the perfectly preserved Mausoleum of Sextus. And, at the same time, odd artifacts and tombstones were continually surfacing from the site of the town.

Which is no doubt why all of these were to be mentioned repeatedly in his later prophecies.

In 1519, when Michel was 16, he was sent to college at Avignon, where a Medical Faculty had been in operation for the past nine years. Whether

ABOVE: *Inspired by his classical education, the young Nostredame was a keen visitor to the ruins of Glanum, an important Greco-Roman city.*

he actually studied the subject there is unknown, though, as is the outcome. An outbreak of the plague forced the suspension of all studies in 1520, so Nostredame may or may not have gained his Bachelor's degree by then. It may seem improbable, but his contemporary, the celebrated writer and scholar François Rabelais, is known to have gained his own degree at Montpellier in as little as six weeks, possibly thanks to previous academic and medical experience.

THE PLAGUE DOCTOR

By his own admission,[44] Nostredame spent the next nine years wandering the countryside in search of medicinal herbs and other cures. In October 1529, now an experienced apothecary, he entered the Montpellier medical faculty to take his doctorate. He was almost immediately expelled from the student body, however, on the grounds that, during his time as an "apothecary or pharmacist," he had been unacceptably rude about the medical profession. Circumstantial evidence suggests that, despite this, he managed to get himself reinstated and continue his studies.[8] Among his fellow students was Rabelais, who enrolled there the following year.

A plague doctor wearing protective clothing. At the same time as Nostredame was a medical student at Avignon, the "Black Death" was cutting a swathe through France, bringing his studies to an abrupt halt.

On graduating, Nostredame continued his wanderings in the southwest of France, taking in Carcassonne and Bordeaux, before eventually settling down to practice at Agen under the shadow of the prominent, if cantankerous, philosopher, doctor, and all-round scholar Julius Caesar Scaliger. By around 1535, however, he had left again, having lost not only his first wife, Henriette d'Encausse, but also their two children to some unspecified epidemic. Apparently under pressure, not only from her family but also from the Inquisition of Toulouse – whom he had seemingly offended with an incautious remark, to say nothing of the ever-vituperative Scaliger himself – he again took to the road, traveling all over France and possibly farther afield, too.

In 1544 he turned up in Marseille, where he proceeded to assist the eminent physician Louis Serre in his fight against the current plague epidemic. He was then summoned to Aix-en-Provence to take personal charge of a further

outbreak there. By 1547 he was practicing in Salon-de-Provence where, after a brief absence to fight yet another epidemic at Lyon, he finally settled down and married for the second time – this time to a rich widow called Anne Ponsarde, also known as "Twinny" (*Gemelle*). They were to have six children, two of whom – César and Charles – would, in due course, achieve considerable local prominence.

PROPHET AND AUTHOR

Before the children started arriving, however, the now semi-retired doctor paid a lengthy visit to Italy, possibly in preparation for his new chosen role in life – that of prophet and sage. Already congenitally endowed on his mother's side (so he claimed) with "the sight," he now proceeded to train himself in a variety of astrological and theurgic techniques designed to refine that gift still farther. The latter, admittedly, involved "summoning up spirits," but the former posed absolutely no contradiction for the ex-doctor: physicians were routinely trained in astrology for diagnostic purposes.

The upshot was (from 1550) the first of a series of annual *Almanachs*, designed to provide a calendar, a lunar ephemeris (a set of tables), and other astronomical information for the year

After completing his medical studies, Nostredame spent several years working as a physician in southwest France, often during plague epidemics. Despite much recent disinformation on the subject in English-language publications, however, next to nothing is in fact known about his methods.

ABOVE: *After his apprenticeship as a plague-doctor in Marseille, Nostredame was summoned to Aix-en-Provence to fight an outbreak there. Contrary to some modern reports, however, he admitted in his writings that none of his methods worked.*

ahead, together with long-term forecasts for the weather, for agriculture, and for matters both political and military. They increased in detail every year, sold like hot cakes, and were soon exercising an influence even on ruling circles, both at home and abroad.

Other less well-known works flowed from his pen as well. His bestselling cosmetics manual and cookbook, the *Traité des fardemens et confitures* – clearly the fruit of his long practical experience as an apothecary (and, it has to be said, much friendlier than Mrs. Beeton) or indeed, Julia Child – came out in 1555, while an extremely free translation of a work by the ancient Greco-Roman physician Galen followed in 1557.

His early *Orus Apollo*, however, was not published at the time. This was another very free translation, this time in verse, of an obscure and highly ill-informed classical work on the meanings of Egyptian hieroglyphs (Champollion's definitive decoding of the Rosetta Stone – now in the British Museum – was not to appear until 250 years later). Its manuscript, formerly owned by Colbert (Louis XIV's finance minister), and now housed in the Bibliothèque Nationale, Paris (manuscript No. 2594), is clearly written in the self-same hand as Nostradamus's signature on his will and the *ex libris* inscription at the top of his personal copy of Jean Stadius's *Ephemerides*, as illustrated on page 29.

Nature faige mere de Sympathie

Par faictz contraires ce rend Antipathie

A... ... ... par sa concorde

Et la deff... re apres par sa discorde

Comme il me semble chose bien necessaire

Descripre vng peu si se profond mistere

Mefmes les chofes paffant lengin humain

Je n.ay tradnich ces deux limes envain

Mais pour monstrer a gens laborieux

Que aux bones letres se rendent studieux

Part of the first page of Nostradamus's verse translation of the Orus Apollo, *a work on Egyptian hieroglyphs, apparently in his own hand. Note the complete absence of punctuation.*

THE CRITICS

As political and religious troubles started to tear France apart, especially after the sudden death of King Henri II in 1559, the annual *Almanachs* increasingly became the subject of virulent public criticism, both lay and religious. There were tirades by Protestants, who branded him and all his ilk as agents of the devil. There were protests by Catholics at his alleged use of magic. There were attacks by poets for his clumsiness, by laymen for his superstition, and by the local Catholic peasants for allegedly being on the side of the Protestants, and so on.

And not only in France, either. In England, too – where even Queen Elizabeth's Secretary of State Sir William Cecil soon had a copy – Nostradamus (as he now styled himself) quickly became the butt of virulent public pamphlets castigating him for the allegedly subversive religious and political ideas enshrined in his predictions and publications.

At home, the matter reached crisis-point in 1561, when the new-found seer – who was by now investing much of the resulting wealth in a major local irrigation project – was arrested and briefly imprisoned in the castle of Marignane (home of the modern Marseille airport) for spreading inflammatory literature.

But by far the most devastating of the attacks were those from the professional astrologers. Nostradamus, they claimed, simply didn't know what he was talking about. He kept putting planets in the wrong signs. He happily assigned the sun to the wrong part of the sky, or even to two different parts of it at once. He clearly didn't know how to perform the astrologer's primary task of calculating the Ascendant, and hadn't the first idea how to interpolate from the existing tables. More-

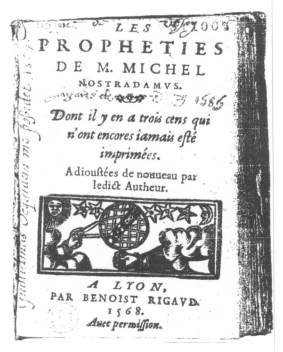

The title page of the first omnibus edition of the Propheties, *published in 1568, and a bestseller ever since.*

over, his claims about what the stars revealed to him went far beyond anything that astrology could possibly say.

To all of this (much of it, alas, entirely justified!) Nostradamus repeatedly came up with a time-honored defense. He was, he said, "divinely inspired." This effectively put an end to all the argument, just as it was of course designed to do.

THE *PROPHETIES*

Meanwhile, by around 1554, Nostradamus had started work on a further project – namely the production of a book of a thousand prophecies arranged in ten books, or *Centuries*, designed to foretell the entire future history of the world up to

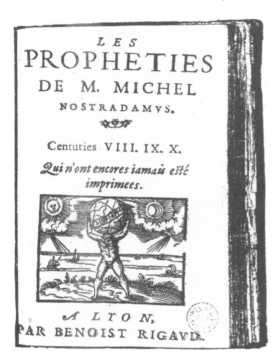

Title page of part 2 of the 1568 Propheties: *they had the ambitious aim of foretelling the future up until the year 3797.*

the year 3797. It was produced in three installments, the first of which came out in May 1555, apparently to mark the first birthday of his infant son César. The second appeared in 1557, and the third (now lost) in 1558. The first omnibus edition appeared posthumously in 1568, though it lacked (as have all editions since) some 58 verses of the original seventh "Century." Translated into numerous languages, the *Propheties*, as they were entitled, have rarely, if ever, been out of print since.

RIGHT: *Nostradamus allegedly predicted the fate of King Henri II of France, killed in a joust by a splinter from a lance.*

The first edition created an immediate sensation. Summoned to the court in Paris that same summer by Queen Catherine de Médicis, the seer was called upon to draw up horoscopes for all seven of her royal children, and was reportedly so appalled by their astrological and medical prospects that he refused to tell her anything other than that "all your sons will be kings."

Both in Paris and after his hasty return to Salon, Nostradamus was soon being consulted by a whole variety of powerful personages, who demanded of him birth-charts, horoscopes, and other astrological readings – though in practice it was normally *he* who asked *them* for their birth-charts, mainly because he was less than confident of his ability to work them out himself. He also conducted a lively correspondence, mainly in Latin (copies of some 51 pieces of which survive), with a number of more remote clients, particularly in Germany. His influence at court meanwhile remained immense, especially after the dramatic death in a tournament of King Henri II, which Nostradamus claimed to have predicted.

ROYAL HONORS

In 1564, less than two years before his death from dropsy on July 2nd, 1566, Nostradamus was visited at Salon by none other than Henri's successor, the young King Charles IX, who was on a nationwide royal "publicity tour" with his powerful mother. During the course of the visit the seer reportedly "discovered" amid the vast royal retinue the young boy who would in due course become the future King Henri IV of France in 1589.

The old sage was then summoned to meet the royal party again at Arles, where he was granted letters patent officially appointing him Royal Councilor and Physician-in-Ordinary to the King, and granted a pension to match. Apparently he was also invited to recommend the marriage of the adolescent Charles to Queen Elizabeth of England, who was twice his age. She eventually replied, in characteristic vein, "My Lord is too great for me, and yet too small."

The final resting place of Nostradamus's bones in the Collégiale St.-Laurent in Salon.

And so it was that his confident prophecy, published in his subsequent 1566 *Almanach*, that the great royal wedding would take place in May 1567 failed resoundingly. So, indeed, did a number of other predictions in the same *Almanach* — notably his constant warnings of imminent major Muslim invasions of Europe.

Were Nostradamus's prophecies always so fallible, then? And if so, whence the undoubted renown as a prophet that he has enjoyed from that day to this? Does he deserve it?

In subsequent chapters we shall be examining these questions more closely.

LEFT: *The modernistic "Monument to the Spirit of Nostradamus" in today's Salon-de-Provence.*

OPPOSITE: *Nostradamus is famous for his alleged "discovery" of the future Henri IV during the royal visit to Salon of 1564. (Detail from painting by L. Denis Valverane.)*

THE METHOD REVEALED

Ever since ancient Babylonian times, astronomers had been wrestling with the possible significance of astronomical cycles. Lineups of most or all the planets in the same sign of the zodiac were generally supposed to be omens signaling the imminent destruction of the world by fire or flood. Other, lesser conjunctions boded all kinds of fateful events, too. And in Nostradamus's day the whole thing was further complicated by attempts to link such ideas with a supposed 7000-year destiny for the world, counting from the date of the biblical Creation. Superimposed on this was a complicated medieval system of theoretical "ages" each lasting 353 years and 4 months, each governed by a different planet, and each supposedly ruled over by a different angel or archangel.

All these concepts were to be duly mirrored in Nostradamus's writings, but it was the major planetary lineups that seem to have done most to spark his interest and lead directly to his prophetic career.

THE GREAT CONJUNCTION OF 1524

As it happened, just such a major alignment occurred in February 1524, during his early years as a wandering apothecary, when all the then-known "planets," including the sun but excluding the moon, lined up dramatically in Pisces.

What, then, happened as a result? Absolutely nothing of any consequence. And indeed, looking back at the last occasion when a similar conjunction had happened in 1186, nothing of any consequence had happened then, either (I have published charts for both occasions in my *Nostradamus Encyclopedia*). Nor, for that matter, had anything happened the time before that, in 710 C.E.

Possibly the young Nostredame had already done the research and realized this fact. And possibly he had deduced that, as a consequence,

A traditional horoscope prepared by Nostradamus in July 1552 for Prince Rudolf Maximilian, one of many rich and powerful clients who sought his advice.

nothing would happen this time either. Perhaps he had even stuck his neck out and said so openly.

If so, he was proved right. Possibly then, he had taken the first step in his prophetic career. *By looking back at the past, he realized, he could actually hope to predict and time future events.*

The next year, however, disaster struck. Not only did France's armies suffer a huge and bloody defeat at Pavia in Italy, but King François I and his two sons were captured and held to ransom. And, to cap it all, a huge plague epidemic started to sweep the south of France.

No doubt the young apothecary hurriedly consulted his books again – only to discover that similar disasters had indeed followed the previous alignments, both of them involving major Muslim victories over Christendom. In the year 711 the Moors had invaded Spain, and in 1188 Saladin had succeeded in destroying the Crusader kingdoms in the Middle East.

Was there, then, some kind of delay-mechanism built into the system? If so, then Nostradamus could add a further rule to his developing prophetic technique. *Planetary alignments tended to time the "causal" periods leading up to events, and not the events themselves.*

During Nostradamus's lifetime outbreaks of plague were common and caused widespread fear and suffering.

*The Copernican system of the universe, with the Earth
and other planets revolving around the Sun.*

EXTENDING THE SYSTEM

But now a further consideration seems to have sprung to Nostradamus's mind. Thus far, only straight-line planetary arrangements had been involved. But what if the same applied to *any* planetary pattern, straight-line or not?

If so, then all he would have to do in order to predict and date the repetition of some ancient event would be to look up the positions of the planets at the time and calculate just when the self-same pattern of planets would recur – whether straight-line or otherwise. Indeed, by comparing the declination (i.e. height) of the sun at noon on the two occasions it might even be possible to adjust the original latitude in such a way as to calculate that of the future event, too.

It was childishly simple. All that was needed, in fact, was a reliable source of astronomical data. And, as luck would have it, this was readily to hand and accessible to Nostradamus.

THE AVAILABLE DATA

Ever since about 1540, astronomers and astrologers (at the time, these were really one and the same) had been publishing comprehensive tables with just this kind of eventuality in view. There were books and sets of tables from a whole range of writers – not least the celebrated Nicolaus Copernicus (finally published in 1543). One of them, Petrus Apianus, even went so far as to supply a kind of rotary cardboard computer with his book (rather like the crude device formerly supplied to pilots for navigating on their knees), so that readers could calculate just which planets would be in which signs for centuries ahead.

Many of them jumped at the chance. And so it was that by 1549, simply by using the figures supplied, the astrologers Pierre Turrel and Richard Roussat between them were able to predict a major planetary alignment for 1789, and to warn the world of a huge social and political upheaval for that year. In effect, they successfully predicted the French Revolution *over 200 years ahead of time!*

In Nostradamus's day, astrologers and astronomers were one and the same.

For Nostradamus, clearly, it was an exciting prospect. The principle was there. The data was there. All he had to do now was to retire from medicine and put them to work.

And so in 1547 that was precisely what he did.

The upheaval of the French Revolution began in 1789, as predicted by astrologers well over 200 years earlier.

THE NEW CAREER

Admittedly, having just married for the second time, Nostradamus first set out on a trip to nearby Italy. One can imagine that Florence, with its wealth of ancient documents (including astronomical records), may well have been his major destination. By the time he returned in around 1549 or 1550 he was set to embark on his new career as a professional prophet.

We can still see the consequences. Almost at once his long series of annual *Almanachs* started to appear. Within a year or so Madeleine, the first child of his second marriage, appeared too. And within five years his first book of prophecies for the future of the world – the *Propheties* – successfully saw the light of day.

EVIDENCE

The mere fact that Nostradamus
constantly employed characters from classical antiquity
to act as players in his prophetic scenario – Jason,
Hannibal, and Nero among them – is evidence enough
that he expected the ancient past to repeat itself in the
future. Moreover, in the two letters that accompanied
his first and final editions, he as good as said that it
was the recurrence of particular planetary configurations
that governed that repetition. No doubt that was why
Chavigny, his secretary, later published a book describing
him as *The French Janus* - Janus being the Roman god
who looked both forward and backward at once.

COMPUTERIZED EVIDENCE –
THE ACCESSION OF AUGUSTUS

It is no surprise, then, to find computerized astrology programs backing up the idea. My published translation of verse X.89, for example, reads as follows:

> *Brick walls they shall in marble reconstruct:*
> *Of peace seven years and fifty shall there be.*
> *For humans joy: rebuilt each aqueduct:*
> *Health, honeyed times, and rich fecundity.*

Now this clearly refers to the words of the Emperor Augustus who, looking back over what he had done for Rome during his 57-year stewardship of the city, is said to have boasted that he had "found it brick and left it marble." On this basis, then, Nostradamus was clearly predicting a future 57 years of comparable peace and prosperity – and so it ought to be possible to calculate just when it is due by referring to the planetary positions at the time of, or a few weeks prior to, the Emperor's accession. Inspection of the astrological data in fact suggests that the period in question is dated to 1945 to 2002 – or possibly 2037 to 2094, when the planets next align in the same way.

Or at least those are the *current and the next dates* for its recurrence. This of course is a point that it is always vital to remember with Nostradamus's astrological datings. Astrology is essentially cyclic. And so any given planetary pattern is liable to come around again and again over the course of the centuries – more frequently in the case of the inner planets, less frequently in the case of the outer ones with larger orbits.

Certainly, however, there has been a corresponding period of peace and growing prosperity in Europe ever since 1945 – even though, following the widespread mass bombings of the Second World War, the seer's predicted reconstruction in *white marble* actually turned out to be mainly in buildings of *white concrete*.

The Delphic oracle, which Nostradamus used as a model for his own divinatory practices (see next chapter). The priestess inhaled the vapors from the water, rather than gazing into it.

Nostradamus studied the planetary patterns accompanying great events of the past, predicting that they would happen again when these patterns recurred in the future. He seems to have taken the planetary configuration at the time of the conception of Emperor Augustus and applied it to that of a future world leader in 2012 – namely "Henri V" of France.

THE FUTURE HENRI V OF FRANCE

Exactly the same *caveat* applies when Nostradamus comes to foretell the French king who is apparently due to reign over the next mini golden-age of 57 years as a kind of latter-day Augustus. Nevertheless, the planetary positions for each of those occasions are quite definite, and can be illustrated very simply. For doing so I like to use a pair of what I call *horographs* – simplified charts showing only which planets are in which signs of the zodiac, with planetary positions that are common to both charts printed in blue.

Verse IV.93, for example, clearly refers to Suetonius's well-known depiction (apparently borrowed from the much older birth-myth of Alexander the Great) of Augustus's conception as the result of the coupling of a snake with his mother near the temple of Apollo.[15] In my translation, Nostradamus's verse reads:

> *A dame shall see a snake at night advance*
> *Upon the royal bed. No dog shall cry.*
> *Then shall be born a royal prince in France*
> *Whom all kings see as sent from heaven on high.*

Augustus, having been born on September 23rd, 63 B.C.E., must have been conceived at around the beginning of the year. Taking the horograph for a few weeks prior to Augustus's conception, therefore, the positions of the planets for the event's "causation" might be taken to be as in the top horograph opposite.

In order to find out just when Nostradamus's anticipated future "king of the world" is likely to be born, therefore, we merely have to establish when the planets will once more take up similar positions. A possible match is that for the period from December 12th to 16th, 2012 (see bottom chart opposite), when the planets depicted in blue will once again be in the same signs. The comparative latitude suggests that the conception of *Chyren* (as Nostradamus elsewhere calls him) could take place between Madrid and Naples.

HOROGRAPH FOR: November 24th, 64 B.C.E.   **TO:** December 4th, 64 B.C.E.

	Aries	Taurus	Gemini	Cancer	Leo	Virgo	Libra	Scorpio	Sagit.	Capri.	Aqua.	Pisces
Pluto			★									
Neptune				★								
Uranus			★									
Saturn	★											
Jupiter			★									
Mars							★					
Venus								★				
Mercury									★			
Moon	★	★							★	★	★	★
Sun									★			

Solar noon declination (to nearest degree): 21° to 22°S

Geographical latitude: 41° 54'N.

LOCATION: Rome

EVENT: Conception of Augustus (Polizzi p.56) -v.IV.93

HOROGRAPH FOR: December 12th, 2012   **TO:** December 16th, 2012

	Aries	Taurus	Gemini	Cancer	Leo	Virgo	Libra	Scorpio	Sagit.	Capri.	Aqua.	Pisces
Pluto										★		
Neptune												★
Uranus	★											
Saturn								★				
Jupiter			★									
Mars									★			
Venus								★				
Mercury									★			
Moon									★	★	★	★
Sun									★			

Solar noon declination (to nearest degree): 21° to 22°S.

Geographical latitude: 41° 54'N.

POSSIBLE LOCATION: Madrid to Naples

EVENT: Conception of new "ruler of the world" (Henri V?)

The great Donati Comet of 1858. The appearance of comets was often seen as a portent of disaster.

As we shall see, the suggested dates fit Nostradamus's apparent chronology for the near future with great aptness.[33] Even the choice of locations fits the seer's apparent expectation that the future Henri V (*Chyren* has always been recognized as an anagram of *Henryc*) will eventually be married *in Spain*:

> *The year that Saturn shall withdraw his writ*
> *Shall Frankish lands by floods be stricken hard.*
> *With Trojan blood a marriage he shall knit,*
> *While Spaniards shall provide a bodyguard.*

THE FUTURE "MABUS"

But Nostradamus evidently considered much more recent (and even contemporary) events to be ripe for this treatment, too. A notable case in point is his celebrated prediction at II.62 of the death of one "Mabus," leading to terrible bloodshed and vengeance, and marked by a comet in the sky. Duly allowing for the seer's somewhat arch substitution of *cent, main* for the obvious words *sang humain* in the final line, my published translation of the verse[33] reads as follows:

> *Mabus shall shortly die. Then shall ensue*
> *Of man and beast a laying waste most dread.*
> *Then suddenly shall vengeance heave in view:*
> *Thirst, famine, blood, with comet overhead.*

Notwithstanding the widespread modern tendency to assume that Mabus is to be some kind of future Antichrist (a seductive tradition by which I admit to having allowed myself to be bamboozled in the past), the historical precedent is in fact much more humdrum. Intriguing though it may be that the last U.S. ambassador to Saudi Arabia was one *Raymond E. Mabus*, and that a judicious use of mirrors can make *Mabus* look just a little like *Sadam*, the *historical* Mabus (or rather, Mabuse) was in fact no more than a humble Flemish painter. Born in Maubeuge (or Mabuse) in modern France, in around 1472, Jan Gossaert de Mabuse (who liked, after the classical tradition of the day, to style himself "Malbodius") studied under both Leonardo da Vinci and Michelangelo, and is best known for his typically Renaissance religious paintings. He died in Breda (in modern Holland) on October 1st, 1532.

There really can be little doubt that it is to Mabuse's death that Nostradamus is referring in his celebrated quatrain. For the accompanying events were precisely as described. It was in this same year that the forces of the Emperor Charles V finally managed to push back the ravaging Muslim hordes of the invading Ottoman empire from before the very gates of Vienna – temporary though the respite was to prove – and, as though to set the seal on this long-overdue piece of European "own-back," the year was also marked by a particularly bright daylight comet.

Both the date and the sequence of events are therefore well known. So are the latitudes both of Mabuse's death and (to within broad tolerances) of the ensuing Western victory over the Muslims. According to Nostradamian logic, therefore, it ought to be possible to pinpoint both the date and the latitude of their future repetition. And so, indeed, it turns out to be. The relevant horographs are pictured overleaf.

Consequently it turns out that the new "Mabus" is likely to be a prominent painter who dies, probably at Gerona in Spain, in October or early November 2002, and that his or her death will be the signal for a massive (if temporary) repulsion of massed Muslim invaders *in Portugal, somewhere south of Lisbon.*

ABOVE: *"Venus and the Mirror" by the early sixteenth-century Flemish painter Jan Gossaert de Mabuse.*

LEFT: *Numerous modern commentators have tried to link the names "Mabus" and "Saddam" (which they suggest is the name reversed). Unfortunately this is merely an example of the obsessive wishful thinking that surrounds the interpretation of Nostradamus.*

HOROGRAPH FOR: September 14th, 1532   **TO:** December 18th, 1532

	Aries	Taurus	Gemini	Cancer	Leo	Virgo	Libra	Scorpio	Sagit.	Capri.	Aqua.	Pisces
Pluto										★		
Neptune												★
Uranus				★								
Saturn				★								
Jupiter								★				
Mars							★					
Venus								★				
Mercury							★					
Moon	★	★										★
Sun							★					

Solar noon declination (to nearest degree): 1° to 2°S.

Geographical latitude: 51° 35'N.

LOCATION: Breda, Netherlands

EVENT: Death of Jan Gossaert de Mabuse (Malbodius). Flemish painter

---

HOROGRAPH FOR: October 18th, 2002   **TO:** October 29th, 2002

	Aries	Taurus	Gemini	Cancer	Leo	Virgo	Libra	Scorpio	Sagit.	Capri.	Aqua.	Pisces
Pluto									★			
Neptune											★	
Uranus											★	
Saturn			★									
Jupiter					★							
Mars							★					
Venus								★				
Mercury							★					
Moon	★	★										★
Sun							★					

Solar noon declination (to nearest degree): 10° to 12°S.

Relative latitude: 9° to 10°S.   **Geographical latitude:** 41° to 42°N.

POSSIBLE LOCATION: Valença de Minho, Portugal – or Gerona, Spain

EVENT: Death of prominent artist followed by repulsion of Muslim invaders south of Lisbon

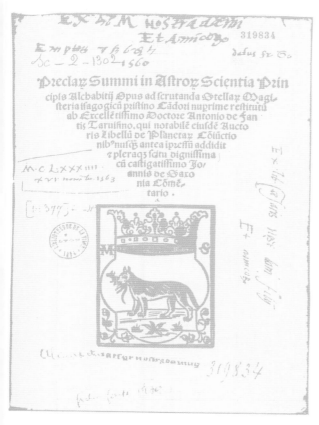

same technique to "date" many of the predictions on which the seer himself, for reasons of self-preservation, was unwilling to put too precise a figure. All that is required, in fact, is that we identify the original historical event on which he based each prediction – even though this will demand a good deal more knowledge of classical history than is common today, or even easily accessible via encyclopedias.

At the same time, of course, we are now in a position to test the technique by actually trying it out for ourselves – identifying major events *since* the prophet's death and predicting, on the basis of computerized astrology-programs, when and where they are likely to recur. Part 2 of this book, indeed, is devoted specifically to this stimulating, if risky exercise in do-it-yourself prophecy.

REUSING NOSTRADAMUS'S OWN
TECHNIQUE TO DATE HIS PROPHECIES

And so Nostradamus's basic technique is revealed for what it is – unduly credulous, some might think, in respect of its presumed links between celestial and earthly events, yet a good deal more scientific and strictly mathematical than the purely magical rigmarole that most commentators attribute to him.

Given his distinctly dubious mathematical and astrological abilities, it is true, Nostradamus's likely accuracy might be questioned. Yet there can be little doubt now about how he worked. This therefore means that we ourselves can hope to use the

NOSTRADAMUS'S OTHER TECHNIQUES

Comparative horoscopy was far from being Nostradamus's only prophetic technique. His constant claims of divine inspiration were based on the idea that the planets were merely physical manifestations of the classical gods after whom they were named, and that these in turn were merely particular expressions of the Supreme Godhead itself. Having carefully prepared himself by a process of prayer and calming meditation, he also claimed to be able to contact such gods and spiritual entities *directly* via a battery of further techniques.

OPPOSITE:

A 19th-century engraving of an anonymous old man, often supposed to be Nostradamus.

The ancient Greek philosopher, Iamblichus of Chalcis, who described the oracles of his time.

THEURGY

Theurgy is the ritual summoning up of gods and/or spirits – generally in order to gain information from them, such as details of future events – and the very first two verses of Nostradamus's *Centuries* are a free translation from the classic work on the subject. This was the *De Mysteriis Aegyptiorum*, written by the third- to fourth-century neo-Platonist philosopher Iamblichus of Chalcis, whose originally Greek text was readily available in Latin in Nostradamus's day (though he in fact knew both languages). Indeed, since it was one of the seer's own future publishers who reprinted it in Lyon in 1549, it is not impossible that this reprinting was at his personal behest. Practical instructions for putting theurgy into effect were and are to be found in the classic magical *grimoire* – the *Clavicula Salomonis*, or "Key of Solomon."

In the course of his work, Iamblichus describes how the female oracles of the ancient Greek temples at Colophon, Delphi, and Branchidai (now Didymi in Turkey) prepared themselves, induced their trances, and were taken over by their respective gods. He describes, too, how each type of spiritual entity can be recognized, controlled, and commanded by the oracle.

And, sure enough, verse 1 of the *Centuries* describes the seer as he attempts to reproduce the Delphic rite, and verse 2 that of Branchidai (which he mentions by its Latin name of *Branchis*). These are slightly edited versions of my previously published translations:

> I.1
>
> *Seated, at ease, the secret eremite*
> *On brazen tripod studies through the night.*
> *What 'midst the lonely darkness flickers bright*
> *Bids fair to bring what none should doubt to light.*
>
> I.2
>
> *Wand placed in hand as once in Branchis' fane,*
> *He dips in water both his hem and feet.*
> *A dread voice shakes him in his gown amain,*
> *Then light divine! The god assumes his seat.*

The brazen tripod, the tiny flame amid the darkness, the ritual wetting of hem and feet, the external presence of the God – all reproduce exactly the details of Iamblichus's account.

In his accompanying letters, too, Nostradamus constantly stresses the dual approaches of astrology and theurgy, while disclaiming for himself all personal claims to being a prophet on his own account. The job of theurgy, it seems, was to add color and detail to the predictions already arrived at via astrology (see previous chapter).

INCUBATION

Incubation is basically the process of "sleeping on a problem," though in this case in a highly ritualized context. It is designed to produce inspired dreams, and in Nostradamus's case led to what he claimed was a kind of "automatic writing." While in sleep or trance, in other words, the god involved actually dictated to him what he was to write.

Although there is no mention of this process in his *Propheties*, it is fully described in his private correspondence, which contains three of the resulting oracular poems. Curiously, though, all three are in carefully constructed Latin, while at the same time offering acrostics (texts whose letters read both vertically and horizontally) on the seer's own name and that of one of his clients.

This could suggest that the seer's real inspiration was the linguistic framework that these acrostics offered, rather than the claimed celestial intervention revealed through sleep.

ABOVE: *Nostradamus may have used trance techniques for writing his prophecies.*

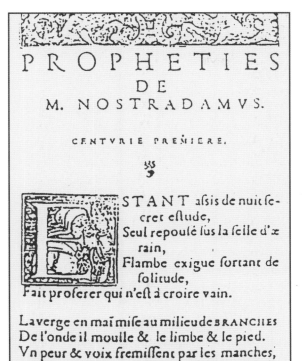

The 1555 edition of the Propheties: *first two verses.*

LANGUAGE

There is plenty of evidence that Nostradamus found inspiration in language itself – which, he would have argued, was similarly God-given. The mere fact of writing his prophecies in regular French shaped and modified at the outset what was said. Lines had to rhyme, words had to fit, syllables had to add up. Often the skilled linguist can spot the resulting use of abbreviations and less-than-ideal substitute words and rhyming syllables, especially in the last line of a verse. Nostradamus may have been a seer, but often he couldn't even see the end of a verse coming!

SCRYING

Numerous recent popular accounts claim that Nostradamus used the process of scrying – gazing into a bowl of water – to gain further insights into the future. Films and videos even represent him doing it. However, there is no mention of this anywhere in his writings. The tradition probably goes back to a garbled understanding of the two verses quoted above. The twin mentions of the words "tripod" and "water" have led commentators to assume that it was the water that was on the tripod, rather than the prophet himself. This is entirely at variance with the practice both at Delphi and at Branchidai. Here it was the priestess or seer who sat on the tripod, while the water was used for ritual cleansing and aromatic purposes.

The ancient Greek oracles, like that at Delphi,
used trance to transmit the prophecies of the god of
the temple to those asking for insight.

MAGIC MIRRORS

This similarly popular tradition (which has even been illustrated in engravings) once again goes back to a confused understanding of what Nostradamus says. In his covering letter to King Henri II, Nostradamus explains that his visions came to him "as in a burning mirror." In fact, a *mirouer ardant* was simply a concave mirror used by alchemists and others for collecting and focusing the sun's rays – so anybody who has ever looked into a simple shaving mirror will know exactly what Nostradamus meant by this!

An engraving of Catherine de Médicis with her astrologer, sometimes thought to be Nostradamus, but more likely to be Cosimo Ruggieri, Catherine's Italian magician and chief familiar.

TESTING THE TECHNIQUE

Undoubtedly the best way to test a theory of how an ancient prophet worked is to try his techniques for yourself. This, consequently, is what I have attempted in Part 2 of this book.

The results of comparative horoscopy, the benefits of "sleeping on a problem" (albeit not, in my case, with any particular ritual preparation), and especially the influence of the verse-form itself – all of these had enormous effects on the outcome. The fact that I did not choose to apply Nostradamus's theurgic techniques for myself ought to have produced clear and identifiable differences between Nostradamus's resulting verses and my own predictions.

And indeed it did. Nostradamus's turned out to be much more detailed, much more colorful, and much denser – clearly suggesting that, as a result of his theurgic practices, he had more information to impart in his four short lines.

Or rather in his eight – for there is plenty of evidence that most of his verses were written in pairs – albeit generally widely separated ones. I have therefore carried on this tradition in my own efforts to reproduce his technique.

The main basis for the prophecies set out in Part 2, however, is honest-to-goodness comparative horoscopy, just as it undoubtedly was in Nostradamus's case. My computer-assisted calculations reveal – just as Nostradamus's clearly did – that there are clear periodicities in the movements of the planets. These tend to congregate around the 240- and 960-year marks, but there are shorter-term sub-loops as well. A notable one is the triple 59-year loop that, for any given planetary pattern, appears to set in every few centuries and then drift out of sync again.

On May 6th, 1937 the German airship Hindenburg *burst into flames while approaching its mooring post at Lakehurst, New Jersey.*

This became particularly obvious when I was researching the possible date for the repetition of the now-famous crash of TWA flight 800 with 230 victims just off New York on July 18th, 1996. Scarcely had I composed the relevant verses (for the record, VII.20 [13] and VII.55) than it occurred to me that there seemed to be something horribly familiar about them. Then I realized what they reminded me of. It was the celebrated wreck of the airship *Hindenburg* at Lakehurst, New Jersey in the late 1930s.

Looking up the exact date, I soon discovered the worst. *The* Hindenburg *disaster had indeed happened in 1937, just 59 years previously!*

And indeed, the horoscopic details all matched (see overleaf). Not merely the circumstances and dates (subject to the usual run-up period, which was longer in the case of TWA 800 and so suggested a problem that had been building up for a long time), but the relevant latitudes, too. This particular factor, of course, helps to explain why the place-names in any one of Nostradamus's verses tend to fall within well-defined latitude bands.

By natural extension, then, the events of 1998–9 ought theoretically to reflect – broadly, at least – *what happened in 1939 and 1940.* In which case should we once again expect a rabid dictator whom we thought had been controlled to break out of the straitjacket and threaten the rest of the world? Should we expect a new invasion of neighboring countries, a new declaration of war by the West, a new spread of hostilities all across Europe, the Middle East, and North Africa?

The prospect hardly bears thinking about – yet such possibilities, if valid, need to be faced squarely.

In the following chapters, consequently, we shall be examining the possible implications for the years immediately ahead.

HOROGRAPH FOR: April 26th, 1937				TO: May 5th, 1937							
	Aries	Taurus	Gemini	Cancer	Leo	Virgo	Libra	Scorpio	Sagit.	Capri.	Aqua.	Pisces
Pluto				★								
Neptune						★						
Uranus		★										
Saturn	★											
Jupiter										★		
Mars									★			
Venus	★											
Mercury		★										
Moon								★	★	★	★	
Sun		★										

Solar noon declination (to nearest degree): 14° to 17°N.

Geographical latitude: 40° 01′N.

LOCATION: Lakehurst, New Jersey

EVENT: Wreck of airship *Hindenburg*, with 36 dead

HOROGRAPH FOR: May 3rd, 1996				TO: May 11th, 1996							
	Aries	Taurus	Gemini	Cancer	Leo	Virgo	Libra	Scorpio	Sagit.	Capri.	Aqua.	Pisces
Pluto									★			
Neptune										★		
Uranus											★	
Saturn	★											
Jupiter										★		
Mars		★										
Venus							★					
Mercury		★										
Moon								★	★	★	★	★
Sun		★										

Solar noon declination (to nearest degree): 16° to 18°N.

Relative latitude: 2° to 1°N.   **Geographical latitude:** 42° to 41°N.

LOCATION: Just off New York City, U.S.

EVENT: Explosion of TWA flight 800, with 230 dead, at 40° 40′N.

A computer simulation of the explosion of TWA flight 800 in 1996, which killed all passengers and crew. Was this a repeat of the Hindenburg *disaster?*

CRACKING
THE DATING CODE

The key to discovering what Nostradamus predicted inevitably
lies in arranging his scrambled prophecies in their intended sequence,
so that we can know the true context of each. This in turn means
establishing a basic dating-framework. Fortunately, he offers us
a whole variety of dating-clues to work from.

DATED VERSES

For a start, the seer actually offers what appear to be perfectly normal calendar dates for eight of his prophecies – namely 1580 (VI.2), 1609 (X.91), 1700 (I.49), 1703 (VI.2), October 1727 (III.77), 1792 (Letter to Henri II), 1999 (X.72), and 3797 (Préface to the *Propheties*).

"LITURGICAL" DATINGS

Next, he offers us a variety of dates apparently calculated (as verses VI.54 and VIII.71 specifically suggest) from the universal imposition of the Church's liturgy in 392 C.E. – namely 1996 (*Sixain* 11), 1997 (*Sixains* 12, 14, 16, 18), 1998 (*Sixains* 13, 25, 26, 28), 1999 (VI.54, VIII.71, *Sixains* 21, 23), 2000 (*Sixain* 24), 2001 (*Sixain* 28), 2002 (*Sixains* 23, 26, 42, 44), 2006 (*Sixain* 28), 2007 (*Sixains* 38, 44, 54), 2012 (*Sixains* 24, 54), and 2062 (*Sixain* 53).

ASTROLOGICAL DATINGS

Meanwhile a variety of astrological "fixes" specified within the prophecies offer us a chance to pinpoint, by referring to a planetary ephemeris, at least the *next* occasion on which the associated verses may apply (always bearing in mind, though, that such fixes tend to recur on a cyclic basis). These are to be found at I.16, I.51, I.52, I.83, II.15, II.35, II.48, II.65, II.98, III.96, IV.28 (possibly), IV.29 (possibly), IV.33 (possibly), IV.62, IV.84, IV.86, IV.97, V.14, V.24 (possibly), V.25, V.72 (possibly), V.87, V.93, VI.24, VI.52, VIII.48, VIII.49, VIII.91, IX.19, IX.55, IX.73, X.50, X.67, and *Sixain* 49 (possibly). Of these, the references to a mere single planet are generally no more than an indication of the time of year (see IX.9's "sun in Leo," for example), while more complex references can specify a whole range of possible combinations of months and years.

DATINGS BY COMPARATIVE HOROSCOPY

Given that Nostradamus's basic method involved finding future planetary matches for the horoscopes of major past events, theoretically we should be able to work backward from the resulting prophecies to pinpoint the original dates. Then we should be able to use the planetary positions on those dates to recalculate their future equivalents, so rediscovering their future dates for ourselves in exactly the same way as Nostradamus did.

Unfortunately, however, this presupposes not only a very considerable knowledge of history – and especially of classical history – but also a highly developed ability to "see through" the generalized language of each of the prophecies clearly enough to identify the original event on which it is based. In fact this is not at all easy. All the new prophecies in Part 2 of this book, for example, are based solidly on historical events – nearly all of them from the period since the prophet's death, and many of them from the twentieth century. It is to these original events that the accompanying colored symbols refer. Nevertheless, you may well find that only a handful of them actually ring any bells with you. This seems to be the inevitable result of their being cast in the future tense. Somehow the brain seems to have the greatest difficulty in making the necessary connections with the past, almost as though past and future occupied different mental compartments entirely.

While Nostradamus himself knew perfectly well on which historical events he was basing his prophecies, for us it is inevitably something of a detective trail. In many cases we may well gain

greater success by going directly back to the most likely-looking historical events for ourselves, rather than attempting to work backward from those predicted by Nostradamus. This inevitably runs the risk, though, of reading past events into the prophecies, in much the same way as the less reputable modern commentators often read present and/or expected future developments into them.

Nevertheless, the attempt can be made, especially since it is possible to pinpoint at least some of the original events without too much difficulty. Such an exercise suggests the following tentative connections among others.[32] Bear in mind, though, that the dates listed in the table overleaf represent (as ever) merely the next possible timings for the events in question, rather than fixed and final dates in any absolute sense.

DATINGS BY ASSOCIATION

To all the above it is of course possible to add a whole host of other verses that apparently belong with them by virtue of common themes, personal names or nicknames, place names, time references ("the year after"), and so on. In effect, then, these additional verses can likewise be dated.

PAIRED VERSES

As various commentators have noted, there is some evidence that Nostradamus originally wrote his verses in pairs, rather than singly, thus devoting not four, but eight lines to each topic. Certainly there are many pairs of verses that do seem to belong together, even though they are often widely separated and numbered[32] very differently. This being so, tracing each verse's "pair" ought to make it possible to date up to twice the number of verses already covered by the above.

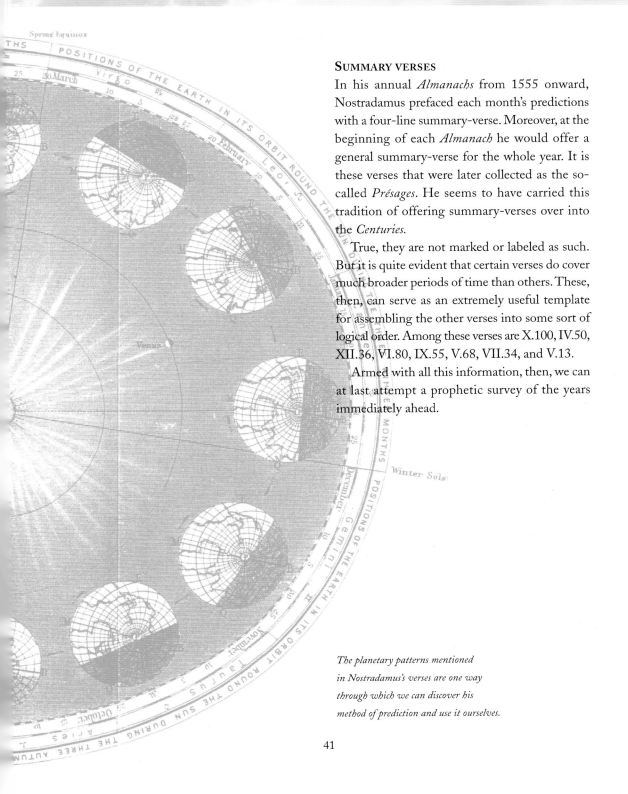

SUMMARY VERSES

In his annual *Almanachs* from 1555 onward, Nostradamus prefaced each month's predictions with a four-line summary-verse. Moreover, at the beginning of each *Almanach* he would offer a general summary-verse for the whole year. It is these verses that were later collected as the so-called *Présages*. He seems to have carried this tradition of offering summary-verses over into the *Centuries*.

True, they are not marked or labeled as such. But it is quite evident that certain verses do cover much broader periods of time than others. These, then, can serve as an extremely useful template for assembling the other verses into some sort of logical order. Among these verses are X.100, IV.50, XII.36, VI.80, IX.55, V.68, VII.34, and V.13.

Armed with all this information, then, we can at last attempt a prophetic survey of the years immediately ahead.

The planetary patterns mentioned in Nostradamus's verses are one way through which we can discover his method of prediction and use it ourselves.

41

Future date	Original date	Relevant prophecies	Future event
1998	1453	III.60	Izmir threatened from the sea by Asiatic forces
1999	480 B.C.E.	Letter, V.25	Huge invasion of western Turkey and Aegean by another "Xerxes"
1999	1429	VI.74, VIII.15	Reemergence of another "Joan of Arc" in northern Britain
1999	579	X.72	Another "Gregory the Great" travels to Sarajevo to buy off Asiatic invaders, but fails: war resumes
1999	1241	V.48, V.54 Présage 31	New "Mongol" hordes sweep into south-east Europe
1999	878	II.4, VII.6, VIII.84, Présage 31	New "Saracen" forces invade Sicily
2000	480 B.C.E.	IX.42	European navies beat off a much larger Asiatic fleet in a new "battle of Salamis"
2000	260 B.C.E.	IX.42, I.37, VI.91	European navies beat off a new "Carthaginian" fleet off Sicily
2000	1396	III.31, V.54	New "Ottoman" Muslim forces invade Armenia
2000	1453	I.40, V.25, V.54, V.70, V.86, VI.21	Forces from Asiatic Turkey overwhelm Istanbul and the Bosphorus
2000	585 B.C.E.	II.86, V.25	Another "Nebuchadnezzar" from Iraq overruns Egypt
2000	870	VI.54, Sixain 19	New "Moors" overrun Egypt
2000	1479	II.5	New "Ottoman" Muslim forces invade southeast Italian mainland
2000	1308	II.41, X.3 VII.22, VIII.99	Pope forced to flee to papal palace at Avignon, France
2002	1517	II.86, V.25	New "Ottomans" overrun Egypt
2002	1532	II.62	Death of a new "Mabus" (painter) presages repulsion of Muslim invaders south of Lisbon (see pages 26–7)
2003	711	II.30, VI.80 Sixain 41	New "Moors" invade Gibraltar from Morocco
2004	1423	II.85, V.81 VIII.6, III.7	Seaborne forces from Spain attack southwest France

Future date	Original date	Relevant prophecies	Future event
2005	472	II.81, IX.99	Volcanic ash from a "new Vesuvius" falls over southern Europe
2005	476	II.93	Last Pontiff ejected from office by foreign invaders
2007	1537	III.20, VI.88	New "Ottomans" invade Spain and North Africa
2010	167	I.72, V.48 *Présage* 31	New invaders from the east attack Danube and/or southern France
2012	1348	I.16, II.6 VIII.21, IX.42	New "Black Death" sweeps Europe from the south
2012	64 B.C.E.	IV.93	Conception of a new "Augustus" – a future "ruler of the world"
2013	1901 B.C.E.	I.87, II.3, II.91, III.7 VI.97, VIII.2, *Sixain 27*	"Fire and brimstone" descend on southern Europe
2015	70 C.E.	II.81, II.93 III.84, IV.82	Sack of "new Jerusalem" (Rome) and burning of "Temple" (St. Peter's)
2019	454	I.52	Rome sacked by new "Vandals" from North Africa
2025	543	I.16, II.37 VIII.17	New "plague" epidemic sweeps into southern France and Spain from the Mediterranean
2027	1017	II.16, II.71	New "Normans" invade "Saracen"-held Italy
2032	49 B.C.E.	II.34, V.23, V.45, VI.7, VI.58, VI.95	Civil war involving a new "Ahenobarbus" sweeps southern France and Italy
2034	190 B.C.E.	II.22, III.64 X.86	A new (European) "Lucius Scipio Asiaticus" defeats the latest (Asiatic) "Antiochus the Great" in the Middle East
2034	1097	I.74, VI.21	A new "First Crusade" invades the Middle East
2036	1535	II.22, I.74, VI.85, II,79, VI.70, VI.27	European forces under a new "Emperor Charles V" invade Muslim heartlands via Turkey
2037	96 C.E.	IV.55	Death of a future "Domitian"
2037	27 C.E.	X.89	Beginning of new "Augustan age" in Europe under new, young ruler

THE NEW MILLENNIUM

Just how far Nostradamus's prophecies for the coming years
should be regarded as fixed and final is a moot point.
From the astrological point of view, certainly, they can represent
only *potential* future events – since astrology is essentially cyclic.
On the other hand, their clairvoyant and theurgic aspects
could suggest that they represent definite events that
Nostradamus could "see" or "hear." Whatever the truth of
it, though, there they now are, and so it behoves us to do our best
to unravel them, making what use we can of the now-decoded
dating-information. And the immediate prospects for humanity,
unfortunately, seem somewhat daunting.

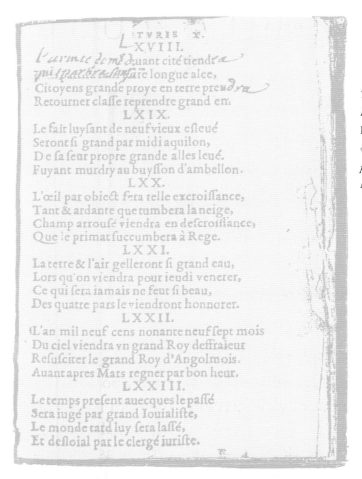

The page from Century X *in Rigaud's 1568 edition of the* Propheties *showing the notorious verse 72 that some have seen as predicting the end of the world, even though it does nothing of the kind.*

THE YEAR 1999

Most speculation about Nostradamus and his prophecies centers around (a) the year 1999 (which he mentions specifically in his notorious verse X.72) and (b) the imminent turn of the millennium (which he doesn't mention specifically at all). However, it has to be said that the usual interpretation of quatrain X.72 bears little relation to what the original French words say.

Above you will see a facsimile of the page on which this verse appeared in its original edition.

You do not have to have X-ray eyes to see that the last word of line 2 is *deffraieur* ("defraying") – not *d'effraieur* ("of terror") as it is usually reprinted.

And so the mysterious figure involved turns out not to be a "King of Terror" after all, still less the coming nuclear explosion, or collision with an asteroid or comet that some "prophetic terrorists" like to suggest. Attempts to link this verse with the "End of the World" and/or the Antichrist, in other words, have to be rejected as the dangerous nonsense they are.

Instead, my latest published translation of the verse reads as follows:

> *When 1999 is seven months o'er*
> *Shall heaven's great Vicar, anxious to appease,*
> *Stir up the Mongol-Lombard King once more,*
> *And war reign haply where it once did cease.*

The process whereby I arrived at this unfamiliar version is fully explained in my *Nostradamus Encyclopedia*.[32] Suffice it to say that the comparative horoscopy reveals that the verse actually refers back to the former Pope Gregory the Great and therefore prefigures not a "King of Terror" but an appeasing Pontiff – presumably the present John Paul II – and his involvement in a disastrous high-level peace meeting on the latitude of Sarajevo.

IMMEDIATE PROSPECTS

Meanwhile Nostradamus appears to assign a number of other events to the years 1998, 1999, and 2000. Some of them can be dated "liturgically," some can be pinpointed (provisionally, at least) by their astrology, and some beg to be dated by comparative horoscopy (see previous chapter).

Thus, there are indications at V.25 of the first signs of a massive invasion of Turkey and Egypt in August 1998 (which, allowing for the usual "causal" time-lag, could mean any time up to the end of September) by an "Arab prince" dubbed the "coiled snake" with "near a million men"; *Sixain* 25 appears to assign to the same year the last visit to Paris of a Chancellor "as big as an ox" who of course begs to be identified with Helmut Kohl of Germany (though Nostradamus offers an alternative date for this of 2001); and at *Sixain* 19 the

seer apparently predicts an enormous increase in militant nationalistic activity among North African Muslims throughout this period.[33]

Other prophecies, too, seem to predict the coming Asiatic and/or Muslim invasion, as the date-list in the previous chapter suggests – while there are indications at verse II.39 of a possible collapse of the European Union during 1999.[33]

By the time you read this you may well know which of these, if any, actually occurred – it was indeed on August 21st, 1998, for example, that Osama Bin Laden duly redeclared his *jihad* on the West – and as a result you will have a better idea of how far Nostradamus's prophecies for the future should be regarded as definite and how far as merely *potential*. In other words, even if these events fail to happen, it might be instructive to ask yourself whether they were nevertheless "in the air" at the time, only waiting for somebody to step in and fulfill them. Ask yourself, too, whether they *did* actually happen, but in unexpected ways. *Was* there an invasion of Europe, for example, but by refugees rather than armed forces?

And you should always bear in mind that Nostradamus himself admitted in one of his letters (though not in those accompanying the *Propheties* themselves) that he could be wrong – not least because God could change His mind!

"God," as he said, "is above the stars."

Which may seem to you a wonderful way of hedging one's prophetic bets – until you realize that the would-be prophet, rather like the weather forecaster, is really on a hiding to nothing. If he is right, and succeeds in warning us of some genuine disaster, we may take steps to prevent it, and so he will be proved wrong – while if he is wrong... he will be proved wrong.

HOROGRAPH FOR: July 24th, 579   **TO:** August 2nd, 579

	Aries	Taurus	Gemini	Cancer	Leo	Virgo	Libra	Scorpio	Sagit.	Capri.	Aqua.	Pisces
Pluto												★
Neptune			★									
Uranus											★	
Saturn											★	
Jupiter				★								
Mars								★				
Venus						★						
Mercury				★								
Moon	★	★	★								★	★
Sun					★							

Solar noon declination (to nearest degree): 19° to 17°N.

Geographical latitude: 40° 54′ to 41° 02′N.

LOCATION: Rome to Constantinople

EVENT: Future Pope Gregory the Great quits Rome to seek help against Lombard invaders

HOROGRAPH FOR: July 19th, 1999   **TO:** July 28th, 1999

	Aries	Taurus	Gemini	Cancer	Leo	Virgo	Libra	Scorpio	Sagit.	Capri.	Aqua.	Pisces
Pluto									★			
Neptune											★	
Uranus											★	
Saturn		★										
Jupiter		★										
Mars								★				
Venus						★						
Mercury				★								
Moon	★	★	★	★	★							★
Sun					★							

Solar noon declination (to nearest degree): 21° to 19°N.

Relative latitude: 2°N.   **Geographical latitude:** 44° to 43°N.

LOCATION: Sarajevo

EVENT: Pope travels to Sarajevo to buy off invaders, but merely stirs them up: war resumes

THE YEAR 2000

Computer-zapping millennium bugs and other obvious nasties apart, most popular speculation about the year 2000 centers around (a) the change of millennium and (b) the dramatic lineup of the planets in Taurus during early May of that year.

However, neither of these, as it happens, is mentioned anywhere in Nostradamus's predictions for future events.

Nevertheless, it needs to be said that since the first year of the first millennium was the year 1 C.E., and that of the second was 1001 C.E., the new millennium will not technically begin until January 1st, 2001. Thus the fears – like the celebrations – have much more to do with the presence of three noughts in the year number than with which millennium we shall be living in. It was ever so. But since the fears and expectations proved totally unfounded on earlier "numerically significant" occasions, there seems to be no more reason why they should be justified this time.

Perhaps it is worth remembering, after all, that for the vast majority of the world's population –

Why is the year 2000 thought so special? Is there any foundation to our fears?

who (being non-Christian) date their calendars from their own "year ones" – the year 2000 will not really be the year 2000 at all.

As for the supposed "lineup" of all the planets (in fact merely the presence of five of them, plus the sun and moon, in the same sign), Nostradamus's own experience as recounted on page 19 should serve as an awful warning. As then, nothing earth-shaking may happen that year at all – though the consequences for 2001 (or possibly 2002) may well turn out, on previous evidence, to take rather surprising forms.

LEFT: *Will the new millennium cause the collapse of our technological cities?*

RIGHT: *Does the "lineup" of five planets in 2000 foretell disaster?*

NOSTRADAMIAN PREDICTIONS
FOR THE NEW MILLENNIUM

As the date-list in the previous chapter reveals, dramatic events will nevertheless be unfolding by then, especially in the Middle East. These I have already outlined in my previous books.[32,33,34] The Asiatic/Muslim invasion already mentioned above will be getting into full swing by the year 2000. Already into both the Balkans and Egypt, it will continue to press westward. In Europe, its massive land and sea irruption into Italy (much aided, it seems, by the carefree vacation atmosphere engendered by celebrations for the new millennium) will result in the Pope's flight to Avignon in France, where he will die toward the end of the year. Within a couple of years France, too, will be invaded from the southeast, at least as far as the river Rhône, and southeast France occupied.

Meanwhile the North African wing of the invasion will soon reach Morocco, whose king will have been deposed and captured by militants as early as 1999. An invasion of southwest Europe via Gibraltar and the Balearics will shortly follow.

With the last Pope ejected from office in around 2005 (despite his disgraceful collaboration with the enemy) the stage will now be set for the final and most terrible act in the drama. Muslim forces from Spain will cross the Pyrenees and, letting loose weapons of mass destruction ranging from the biological and chemical to the thermonuclear, devastate France as they advance northward. The Church especially will be targeted and its priests persecuted. Valiant attempts to stop the advance on the rivers Garonne and Loire will fail, and by

The future Muslim invasion of Europe as apparently foreseen by Nostradamus, after an original by Christopher DeJager.

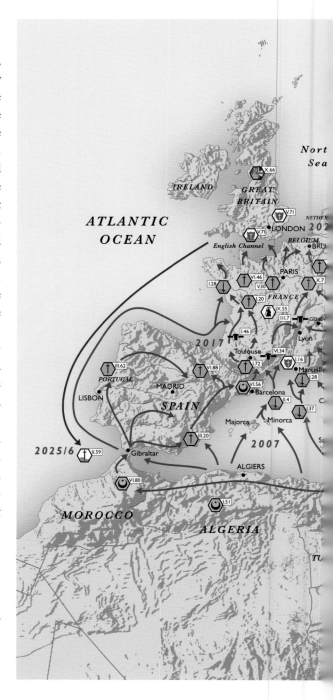

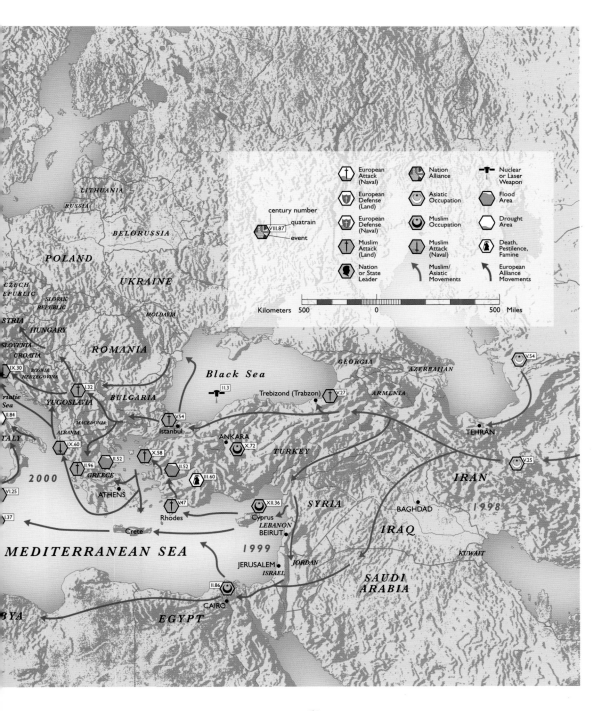

around 2021, with Paris destroyed, the invaders will eventually reach the English Channel and the Belgian border. Chemical and biological weapons will even be aimed across the English Channel at a still largely somnolent Britain.

THE GREAT COUNTERINVASION

Only from around 2026 will a huge counterinvasion be set in train, thanks partly to American help and partly to feuds and divisions within the enemy camp. Following brilliantly planned invasions from both east and west, and an unexpected attack on the Mediterranean coast, the grisly occupiers will be unceremoniously ejected from a ruined France, two-thirds of whose population will by now have died from a combination of warfare, starvation, and disease. In other words, the traditional Four Horsemen of the Apocalypse will be very much at large. Meanwhile grass will be growing knee-high in the city streets, and the field-boundaries will have to be marked out anew as all records of their owners will have disappeared.

Only now will recovery start to take place under a charismatic, if corrupt leader whom Nostradamus dubs "Ogmion" or "Hercules." Eventually Italy, too, will be liberated and abortive attempts made to refound the Church in Rome. But it will be Hercules's successor who – after a brief but ferocious civil war during the early 2030s based on personal rivalry – will finally chase the murderous invaders out of Spain and pursue them back to the Middle East. Named *Chyren* by Nostradamus, and of French royal blood, he will turn out to be the long-awaited King Henri V of France, and under him a new, 57-year period of unprecedented peace, prosperity, and neoclassical civilization will now dawn in Europe from Denmark to the toe of Italy,

despite its tendency (much discouraged at the official level) to resurrect the former pagan cults as well.

FURTHER PROSPECTS

With the arrival of the year 2100, Nostradamus appears to have little else to say that can be pinned down to any particular year – except, of course, to the extent that comparative horoscopy will continue to apply and that former events will consequently tend to continue repeating themselves.

Could it be, then, that it is the future Muslim invasion that is the Big Event he sees coming for us – so big that, after it, there is not too much more to predict? Not much more, that is, apart from the biblical Last Judgment and the end, if not of the world, at least of the present world order (which Nostradamus appears to date to some time during the far-distant twenty-ninth century)? Could the coming invasion be nothing less than the "war of the Antichrist," and the invaders' overlord none other than the Antichrist in person?

There are some signs that Nostradamus thinks so. And yet how reliable is his vision? And how reliable, for that matter, is the interpretation that I have just presented?

THE CRUNCH

Nostradamus himself, remember, admitted that he was not infallible. True, there is a curious Latin phrase in his accompanying letter to the king that reads: *Possum non errare, falli, decepi*. While numerous commentators have assumed that this means "I cannot err, fail, or be deceived," in fact it merely asserts, "It is possible for me not to err, fail, or be deceived." There is, of course, a difference. And since his later letter to the Canons of Orange of February 4th, 1562 reuses the phrase in the form

Humanus sum: possum errare, falli, decepi ("I am human: I can err, fail, and be deceived"), it seems reasonable to infer that the infallibility of Nostradamus should not, after all, be regarded as an article of faith.

In view of this, much hinges on whether certain predicted events come true or not. The key verse is X.72 – the one referring to 1999. Not merely does this bear a clear date, but it seemingly states that war (though only of a generalized kind) will be in progress both before and afterward. Moreover, a whole battery of other verses containing warnings of a huge Muslim invasion seem to be thematically linked to it – quite apart from the fact that four of the verses (two quatrains and two sixains) appear to mention this same date via Nostradamus's "liturgical count," while fourteen of the sixains home in on the period from 1996 to 2012.[32,33]

Much hangs, then, on the "1999" complex of verses. If nothing particularly untoward happens at around this juncture, then what appears to be Nostradamus's main set of predictions for our times falls by the wayside. In which case – despite the inevitability that future commentators will try to explain the fact away by insisting that the seer was "really" counting from some other base-date entirely – we shall have to reassess Nostradamus's claim to be a prophet. The usual claim that Nostradamus was right, but the interpreters wrong, will be very hard to sustain.

But then, who really knows? Such reassessments may prove to be all too agonizingly unnecessary anyway.

What does the future hold for us –
disaster or the prospect of a new dawn? Or both?

par sa con
apres par sa
semble chose
si se profond
choses passant

PART 2

THE NEW PROPHECIES

GUIDE TO THE NEW PROPHECIES

In Part 2 of this book I have experimentally
(if somewhat daringly) presented a further 256 prophecies
of my own to complement Nostradamus's. They are based
on his usual prophetic technique of comparative horoscopy,
but instead use larger, five- or six-planet matches.

Following an arguably over-grand *Prologue* to reflect Nostradamus's first two verses, these 128 pairs of verses each make up a single prediction. As with the seer himself, most of the pairs are split – *but in this case only so that you can calculate the date of each prediction from its two verse-numbers.*

To solve the resulting "puzzle," please proceed as follows:

1 Locate the two verses of any given pair by playing "Snap" with the accompanying symbols. In other words, simply find two sets of symbols that are the same.

2 Next, arrange the two verses that accompany them in the correct order. This is quite simple. The first verse of the pair finishes with a colon: the second finishes (logically enough!) with a period.

V.20   Near Yaroslav they'll sign the final peace   [12]
       Between the mighty lords of East and West:
       Under their armistice all war shall cease,
       All powers be rendered, feuds be set at rest:

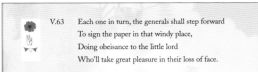

V.63   Each one in turn, the generals shall step forward
       To sign the paper in that windy place,
       Doing obeisance to the little lord
       Who'll take great pleasure in their loss of face.

3 You now have your complete prophecy (in each case the two sets of symbols even give a clue to the *original* event on which it is based).

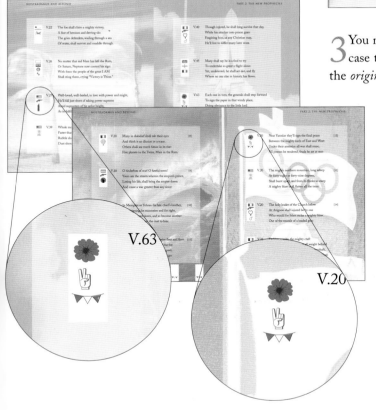

V.63

V.20

4 Finally, read off the *next likely* date for it from the two verse-numbers. The two Roman numerals indicate the months for (a) the beginning and (b) the end of the "period of causation" (normally two or three weeks before the event itself). The Arabic number of the *first* verse gives the first two figures of the year: that for the *second* verse gives the second two figures. [Ignore the figures in square brackets: they are only there to distinguish between similarly numbered verses.] Thus, verses V.20 and V.63 go together to make a prophecy for May 2063.

And enjoy!

PROLOGUE

He takes the stars and every passing planet
And casts them down the corridors of night,
Finds them again as when he first began it
And with them catches history in flight.

He sketches worlds unknown to Nostradamus,
Paints times the ancients never thought to see,
Warns what may benefit and what may harm us,
Shows what may pass, and what must come to be.

He does not claim to be a holy prophet,
Asserts no more than what the planets say,
Sees eons hence and yet thinks nothing of it,
Sees close at hand as every human may.

He does no more than ever man aspired to
When once equipped the figures to compute;
Performs what calculations he's required to,
All claims of special knowledge will refute.

Then, having slept the sleep of incubation,

He'll note what thoughts arise, lest they be missed,

But makes no claim to heavenly inspiration

And any thought of magic will resist.

The former seer, 'tis true, was less resistant

And cultivated all these things and more,

On aid divine especially insistent –

But then what's printed propaganda for?

Take, then, these prophecies as they are offered.

Explore their possibilities at will.

Pair them, then date them with the figures proffered,

And think on them until you've had your fill.

Seek not to change man's future malefactions,

Nor think to thwart the destiny of time:

The outcome of *your* thoughts, *your* will, *your* actions,

Your fears – such is the subject of my rhyme.

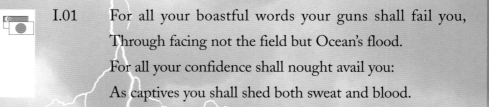 I.01   For all your boastful words your guns shall fail you,

Through facing not the field but Ocean's flood.

For all your confidence shall nought avail you:

As captives you shall shed both sweat and blood.

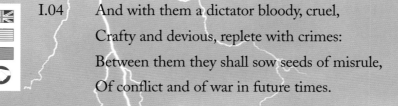 I.04   And with them a dictator bloody, cruel,

Crafty and devious, replete with crimes:

Between them they shall sow seeds of misrule,

Of conflict and of war in future times.

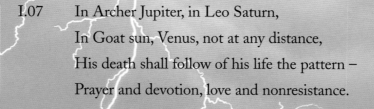 I.07   In Archer Jupiter, in Leo Saturn,

In Goat sun, Venus, not at any distance,

His death shall follow of his life the pattern –

Prayer and devotion, love and nonresistance.

I.10   No matter what he says, they shall not hear him.

They'll take his words and turn them on their head.

No rock to stand on, no one to stand near him:

In public view condemned, beheaded, dead.

I.15   This latter Ludwig, then, who meant no harm,
Who wished for good, yet suffered ill instead,
Who looked but saw not, never raised an arm,
At forty-seven degrees shall lose his head.

I.16   In Libra Neptune, Uranus in Twins,
Sun in Aquarius, Hermes Capricorn,
One culture dies, another one begins.
Death of a man, and yet mankind reborn.

I.20   The little Queen who triply ruled the waves   [1]
Ignored, despised, then worshiped and adored,
Feared the world over by her faithful slaves,
At eighty-two shall go to join her Lord:

I.20   The mighty empire crumbles into dust   [2]
As grave disorder lets the aliens in:
The last dictator goes, as go he must.
Now shall a new regime at last begin:

I.20   With four in Capricorn, the mighty ship   [3]
Shall fall to Earth, nor ever reach the sky.
Parents amazed shall watch them start the trip:
Parents bereaved shall see their children die:

I.20   The final battle shall at last begin   [4]
Near Egypt, where the pyramids still soar,
In twenty-fifty 'gainst the Man of Sin:
From west to east shall spread the grisly war:

I.20   The ancient holy man who speaks of peace,   [5]
And poverty, and closeness to the land
Shall thank not rival creeds for his decease,
But suffer by a cobeliever's hand:

I.20   Hail to the aged bulldog, lord of war   [6]
And guardian of peace, who saved his land,
Thanks to his gift of speech and, what is more,
His passion to inspire and take a stand:

I.20   There at Geneva three shall meet in state   [7]
To parcel out the world in times to come:
One dying cripple beckoned by his fate,
One aging statesman powerless become:

I.20   Look to your guns, Kinshasa, Brazzaville,   [8]
Lest enemies should take you by surprise:
Not from before but from behind they will
O'errun your walls until your city dies:

I.20   A mighty tyrant shall accede to power   [9]
In Dublin or Berlin in 'fifty-one:
By legal means he'll seize the magic hour,
A time of heaven, then hell on Earth begun:

I.21   The great discoverer of worlds uncharted,
A mighty pilot of experience vast,
Shall meet his end wherefrom he once departed
After a quarrel based in actions past:

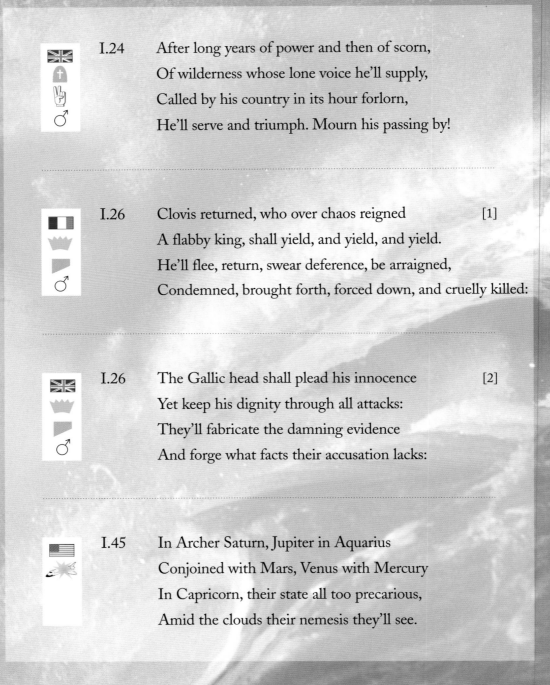

I.24

After long years of power and then of scorn,
Of wilderness whose lone voice he'll supply,
Called by his country in its hour forlorn,
He'll serve and triumph. Mourn his passing by!

I.26 [1]

Clovis returned, who over chaos reigned
A flabby king, shall yield, and yield, and yield.
He'll flee, return, swear deference, be arraigned,
Condemned, brought forth, forced down, and cruelly killed:

I.26 [2]

The Gallic head shall plead his innocence
Yet keep his dignity through all attacks:
They'll fabricate the damning evidence
And forge what facts their accusation lacks:

I.45

In Archer Saturn, Jupiter in Aquarius
Conjoined with Mars, Venus with Mercury
In Capricorn, their state all too precarious,
Amid the clouds their nemesis they'll see.

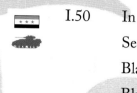

I.50 In Scorpio Mars, and three in Capricorn,
      See vengeance come by night from out the sky!
      Black the avenger, black the rising morn,
      Black sea and land, as Death and War ride by.

I.51 Before the sun from Capricorn shall pass,
      His rule shall be established, and his might:
      None shall suspect his perfidy, alas,
      Nor judge his purposes or plans aright.

II.04 Alas for women and for refugees!
       Alas for all who think the city safe!
       A hundred thousand dead your fate decrees:
       Alas for widow and alas for waif!

II.20 On Alderney, or some such island clime,   [1]
       Her kin, amid a world by turmoil torn,
       Shall see her die and mourn the grievous time:
       Saturn and Jupiter in Capricorn.

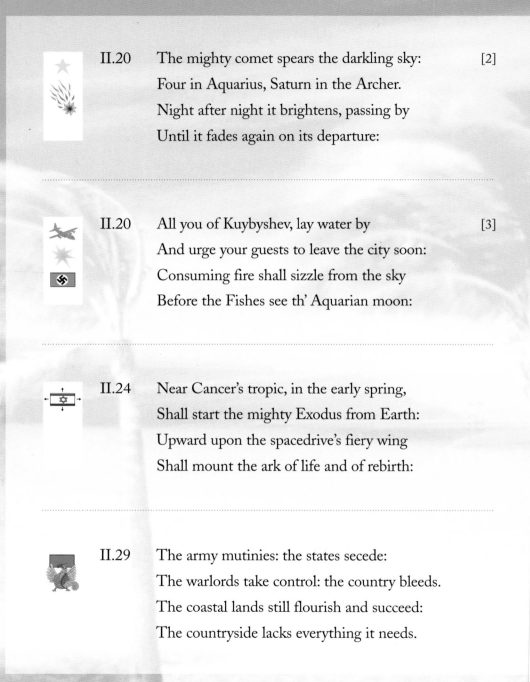

II.20   The mighty comet spears the darkling sky: [2]
Four in Aquarius, Saturn in the Archer.
Night after night it brightens, passing by
Until it fades again on its departure:

II.20   All you of Kuybyshev, lay water by   [3]
And urge your guests to leave the city soon:
Consuming fire shall sizzle from the sky
Before the Fishes see th' Aquarian moon:

II.24   Near Cancer's tropic, in the early spring,
Shall start the mighty Exodus from Earth:
Upward upon the spacedrive's fiery wing
Shall mount the ark of life and of rebirth:

II.29   The army mutinies: the states secede:
The warlords take control: the country bleeds.
The coastal lands still flourish and succeed:
The countryside lacks everything it needs.

II.32 Amid the clouds the mighty Elohim
Shall meet them all, their training to begin:
New miracles and laws they'll learn from Him,
Thereby man's immortality to win.

II.45 What mighty fate can such a sight betoken?
What kings shall die, what governments collapse,
What empires rise and fall, what powers be broken?
Such things could Nostradamus tell – perhaps!

III.04 His wife, his henchmen, hiding underground,
Shall take their lives, fearing to face the foe:
Shells, fighting, fire, and bloodshed all around,
As hell's own ministers to hell shall go.

III.10 And so the lord who would have power supreme,
In his own eyes a god, a mighty hero,
Shall soon be humbled, one whom others deem
A force that's spent, an empty husk, a zero.

III.12   He who killed millions, blighted millions too,
And filled even his closest friends with dread
Shall die – if murdered, poisoned through and through –
Not on some battlefield, but in his bed.

III.14   The Games to distance from Olympia's rhythm,
They'll hold them in an intervening year,
And introduce new laws and customs with them:
No athlete dare half naked now appear.

III.20   The muslin-maker flees the great invasion,   [1]
Flees north, disguised, his mistress by his side,
Then is unmasked, for all his great evasion,
Shot, and strung up as soon as he has died:

III.20   At forty-six degrees, the little Jew   [2]
Who'll overthrow all thoughts of time and space
Shall see the light, and with that light renew
The understanding of the human race:

III.20 The first to plumb the ultimate abyss [3]
Shall circle the vicinity of Earth,
Then shall return from ecstasies of bliss
Rejoicing in humanity's rebirth:

III.20 Long preparation shall precede that flight, [4]
With Jupiter and Saturn in the Goat:
At fifty-one degrees he'll reach the height
At which forever he can float and float.

III.20 At last the mighty tyrant bites the dust [5]
After long years of hideous cruelty:
At last the monster dies, as monsters must.
Alone, untended shall his passing be:

III.20 In March the harbingers of civil war [6]
Shall sweep the south and call the world to arms:
Though no one knows quite what the feud is for
Nor reckons how the fight their country harms:

III.20 The man of God who'll set the world to rights   [7]
Though hated by division's acolytes
At thirty-eight degrees shall meet his end
Because he would his fellow man defend:

III.20 In Ankara the Games they'll found anew,   [8]
But Muslim ones unlike the old tradition.
Of Christian athletes there shall be but few,
Unless by edict, law, or imposition:

III.20 After five years of war, as powers invade,   [9]
He'll be surrounded, in extremity:
Bucharest, Sarajevo, or Belgrade
The mighty leader's suicide shall see:

III.20 In Fishes sun, Venus and Mercury,   [10]
Moon in Aquarius, Fishes, Ram, and Bull –
Such are the signs that shall salvation see
For three adventurers through lunar pull:

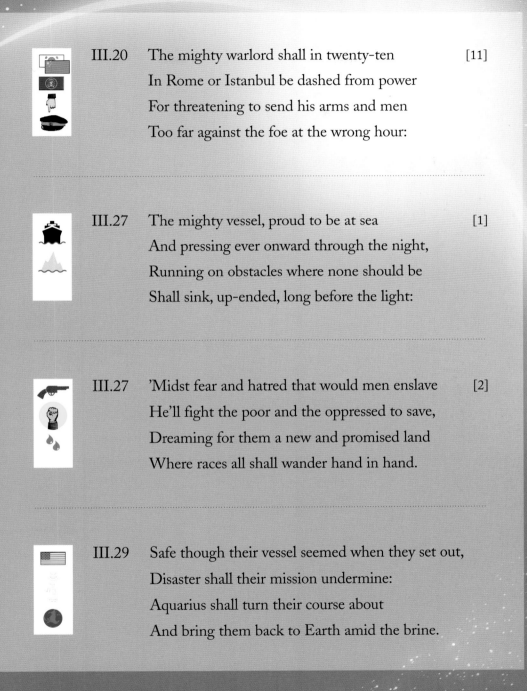

III.20   The mighty warlord shall in twenty-ten   [11]
          In Rome or Istanbul be dashed from power
          For threatening to send his arms and men
          Too far against the foe at the wrong hour:

III.27   The mighty vessel, proud to be at sea   [1]
          And pressing ever onward through the night,
          Running on obstacles where none should be
          Shall sink, up-ended, long before the light:

III.27   'Midst fear and hatred that would men enslave [2]
          He'll fight the poor and the oppressed to save,
          Dreaming for them a new and promised land
          Where races all shall wander hand in hand.

III.29   Safe though their vessel seemed when they set out,
          Disaster shall their mission undermine:
          Aquarius shall turn their course about
          And bring them back to Earth amid the brine.

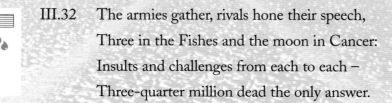

III.32 The armies gather, rivals hone their speech,
Three in the Fishes and the moon in Cancer:
Insults and challenges from each to each –
Three-quarter million dead the only answer.

III.56 He'll father whole new alchemies of thought,
The master of the Nothing and the All:
New worlds shall rise out of the things he taught,
And of old worlds he'll engineer the fall.

IV.04 No more the grand parades, the strutting gait,
The jutting jaw, the ancient might renewed:
There by the Volga he shall meet his fate.
In Crab moon, Saturn; Ram with sun imbued.

IV.19 Volgans, beware the sudden great attack
Across your river, merciless and cruel:
Beware the troops that shall your cities sack,
Loot and destroy your homes for food and fuel:

IV.20   The mighty quake shall half a thousand kill   [1]
At Rome or else Chicago in the spring.
Rebuilding it shall take an act of will,
Yet shall a sense of huge achievement bring:

IV.20   At Aden, or Managua, from the north   [2]
Forces shall come to terminate the war:
The power that once so grandly sallied forth
Shall flee 'midst planes' and helicopters' roar:

IV.20   From Wales to Wicklow they in 'fifty-three,   [3]
Despite delays, disputes, and altercations,
Shall drive a tunnel underneath the sea
To join two different races, tribes, and nations:

IV.20   Latitude fifty-four or fifty-five,   [4]
Fire elemental out of man's control
Shall burst from out its shell as though alive,
Eating men's bodies to their very soul:

IV.23   With eighteen others he'll be cast adrift
By mutineers resentful of his power:
Yet through his competence their hearts he'll lift
And so emerge the hero of the hour:

IV.24   Long shall it be remembered in that clime
How life's unsure and destiny precarious:
Three in the Ram, in Fishes Father Time,
Mars, Neptune, too, and Pluto in Aquarius.

IV.27   The southern island shall a prize await   [1]
That once ruled nations, confident, supreme:
How are the mighty fall'n! What low estate
For him to whom all Earth too small did seem:

IV.27   The mighty chief who freed the sweating slaves   [2]
And forced his will upon a land divided
Shall send untold brave warriors to their graves
But win the day, the battle once decided:

IV.34 No matter that they once did rule so proud
Or try to force their will on humble folk:
The conquerors shall be the common crowd
As they of northern powers the aid invoke.

IV.44 Long the two voyages: the mutineers
An island home shall find, and exile hard:
The captain shall rejoin his former peers,
His name intact, if reputation scarred.

IV.45 Many shall die th' inferno to enchain:
Thousands shall flee to escape its smoke and dust:
On half-a-world away its death shall rain,
Poisoning all who breathe it, drink it must.

IV.53 Sun, Mercury in Aries, two in Taurus,
Pluto Piscean, such shall be the sign
That, though in water, not in strata porous,
Nevertheless the ocean's bed they'll mine.

IV.54 Many the drowned amid the icy deep;
Many the deeds of courage and of fear.
A few shall live their memory to keep.
Sign of an age whose nemesis is near.

IV.66 His enemy defeated he'll forgive
Then, in the evening, go to see a show:
Alas! No longer shall the Great One live
When the assassin aims the deadly blow.

IV.82 The man who once ruled such a mighty realm
Shall be confined in such a little space,
With quite another person at the helm,
As Death ne'er thought to call his dwelling-place.

IV.99 Do all you can to hold the foe at bay:
Withdraw your armies from the other side!
Prepare to be bombarded, blown away,
Starved – but preserve your fortitude and pride!

V.01 There in the northern gulf the fight shall rage,
Each mighty blow a counterblow incite:
The eastern chief unceasing war shall wage
Until the western chief gives up the fight.

V.12 Within four days the news shall reach the world
And grace a coronation great and proud:
The flag that on the mountain was unfurled
Shall fly aloft as choirs shall sing aloud.

V.16 Both north and south, both east and west shall go
To pledge allegiance to a single flag,
Yet troubles and dissensions they shall know:
Quarrels their Babylon apart shall drag.

V.19 Till Holland's ports the last of them shall see, [1]
From Europe Britain shall withdraw its troops:
A fleet of ships, and motor-boats, and sloops
Shall ferry them to safety oversea:

V.19 Kharkov or Kiev, in the year of '99, [2]
Shall be o'errun by forces from the east:
In shall their columns sweep, line after line,
To find that all resistance shall have ceased:

V.20 At forty-nine degrees or forty-eight [1]
What mighty slaughter on the muddy plain!
A million men, cut down by bloody fate,
Shall never see their native lands again:

V.20 From Albion they come, the mighty host! [2]
Vessel on vessel braves the briny deep.
Around Dieppe they'll storm the Norman coast
From alien hordes their neighbors safe to keep:

V.20 Six days the fight shall last, while day and night [3]
The armies head now north, now east, now south:
The city taken, flags upon the height,
The foe chased back beyond the river's mouth:

V.20　　May twentieth in twenty forty-five　　[4]
　　　　After his mighty voyage shore to shore
　　　　Across the ocean, tired but still alive,
　　　　He shall at last arrive at London's door:

V.20　　At last the two shall reach the mountain peak　　[5]
　　　　After so many failures in the past:
　　　　Each to call "first" the world at large shall seek,
　　　　Yet each the other in that role shall cast:

V.20　　In Avignon or Sarajevo they　　[6]
　　　　In spring shall forge a great community –
　　　　A federation built against the day
　　　　When Europe shall become a single see:

V.20　　Flying marauders, creeping in at night,　　[7]
　　　　Shall burst the banks and dams, and flood the plain:
　　　　The Volgans try to shoot them down in flight
　　　　And fail in part, then try and try again:

V.20   Many in disbelief shall rub their eyes   [8]
        And think it an illusion or a scam.
        Others shall see man's future in its rise:
        Five planets in the Twins, Mars in the Ram.

V.20   O tinderbox of war! O fateful town!   [9]
        Yours are the streets wherein the empire's prince,
        Losing his life, shall bring the empire down
        And cause a war greater than any since:

V.20   In Memphis or Tehran the late chief's brother,   [10]
        Campaigning for succession and for right,
        Shall be gunned down, and so become another
        Of his accursed clan the dust to bite:

V.20   Dawn shall see battle joined 'twixt fleet and fleet: [11]
        The flying eyes and ears spy out the foe.
        Each air-attack a hail of fire shall greet,
        Ship after ship down to the bottom go:

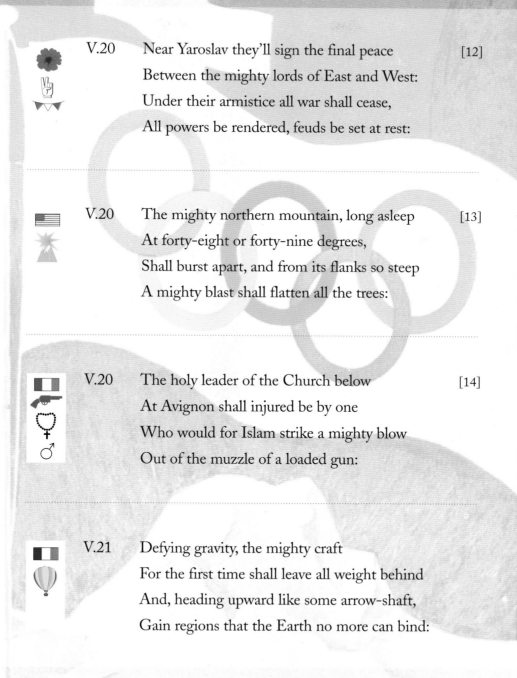

V.20   Near Yaroslav they'll sign the final peace   [12]
        Between the mighty lords of East and West:
        Under their armistice all war shall cease,
        All powers be rendered, feuds be set at rest:

V.20   The mighty northern mountain, long asleep   [13]
        At forty-eight or forty-nine degrees,
        Shall burst apart, and from its flanks so steep
        A mighty blast shall flatten all the trees:

V.20   The holy leader of the Church below   [14]
        At Avignon shall injured be by one
        Who would for Islam strike a mighty blow
        Out of the muzzle of a loaded gun:

V.21   Defying gravity, the mighty craft
        For the first time shall leave all weight behind
        And, heading upward like some arrow-shaft,
        Gain regions that the Earth no more can bind:

V.22   The foe shall claim a mighty victory,
A feat of heroism and derring-do:
The grim defenders, wading through a sea
Of water, shall survive and muddle through.

V.26   No matter that red Mars has left the Ram,
Or Saturn, Neptune now control his sign:
With force the people of the great I AM
Shall sting them, crying "Victory is Thine."

V.27   Well-loved, well-heeled, in love with power and might,
He'll fall just short of taking power supreme
Amid supporters of his ardor bright,
As in fulfillment of some evil dream.

V.39   Whole mountainsides shall move with mighty roar
Faster than any man could hope to flee:
Rubble shall flow the hills and valleys o'er,
Dust shroud the land, the slopes be turned to scree.

 V.40 Though injured, he shall long survive that day,
While his attacker into prison goes:
Forgiving him, as any Christian may,
He'll live to suffer many later woes.

 V.45 Many shall say he is a fool to try
To undertake so great a flight alone:
Yet, undeterred, he shall set out, and fly
Where no one else in history has flown.

 V.63 Each one in turn, the generals shall step forward
To sign the paper in that windy place,
Doing obeisance to the little lord
Who'll take great pleasure in their loss of face.

 V.99 In face of massive odds many shall say   [1]
That 'twas a victory, not a defeat:
Others shall see in such a rank retreat
A chance to fight again another day.

V.99   The government shall flee into the west,   [2]
Most people up and leave as best they may,
The enemy move in to rule the rest,
Yet spare the town to live another day.

VI.03   Again the British cross the ocean sea.
Around St.-Malo they shall come ashore
Their camp to make in deepest Brittany –
Yet southern France shall hear no Lion's roar.

VI.04   Those nations shall not every time agree:
They shall dispute, and argue, and object.
Yet in the end they shall successful be
And every warlike action shall reject.

VI.09   Some shall report a light amidst the sky,
Others a shock, a bang, the earth a-quake.
Many shall wonder what, and how, and why:
Others shall claim no more than a mistake.

VI.20   In Frankfurt, Prague, Cracow, or Kharkov they   [1]
In June shall sign a treaty or a pact
To keep the peace and drive all war away
And punish the aggressor for his act:

VI.20   At thirty-seven degrees and forty-five   [2]
They shall combine to set the world to rights,
Pledged to keep liberty and faith alive,
And universal peace within their sights:

VI.24   Sworn to release the prisoners in the Tower
The city folk shall mill about the walls.
Tumult and fighting till the fateful hour,
Then groans the gate: the mighty bastion falls:

VI.26   The mighty colony shall break away,
The new world claim its freedom from the old:
Together they shall forge another way
And draft a declaration clear and bold:

VI.27 The Gallic Eagle, heading north by east,
Swoops on the angry Lion, now at bay.
The Lion stands his ground, then strikes the beast
And, aided by his minions, wins the day:

VI.28 The mighty meteor from outer space
At sixty-one or sixty-two degrees
Shall devastate the wilderness's face
While laying flat a vast expanse of trees:

VI.32 Once again, Sarajevo, comes the prince
For whom assassins wait, and for his wife:
Then shall six planets join the heavenly Twins
To bring war's storms and mighty loss of life.

VI.34 But once since Alexander's bloody slaughter
At Gaugamela were so many killed
Upon a single day by mud and water
And flying steel and shells with poison filled.

VI.37 And yet too harsh the treaty's terms shall be.
Toothless the guardians of the peace shall seem,
Revenge be in the air, the people flee,
The hoped-for equity remain a dream.

VI.64 The tottering king, his words uncertain, trembles:
His love is strong, but civil strife is stronger.
A new De Launay dies: the mob assembles.
Liberty rules: oppression reigns no longer.

VI.76 Both King and Reaper stand upon the Scales:
Mars rules the Fish. Since Seven combine their art,
Thousands to damn to Hades, nought avails.
The Collie Dog will have his bone apart.

VI.77 In Libra Mars, and Jupiter, and sun,
In Cancer Mercury and Venus met.
From Goat to Fish Earth sees Diana run:
In Fishes Uranus and Neptune yet.

VII.04   No matter that for years he was in power,
Striding the magic stage of history:
No matter that above his age he'll tower –
His time of greatness shall have ceased to be.

VII.06   Yet great disasters shall partition bring,
Huge massacres as people flee en masse:
Too fast the change, too keen to flee the king,
As midnight strikes much, much too soon, alas!

VII.20   At twenty-nine degrees, O King of Kings,   [1]
You'll glory in the land your fathers made:
At twenty-nine, borne off on silver wings,
You'll meet the Reaper as he swings his blade:

VII.20   Like Sodom and Gomorrah once again   [2]
At Tyre and Sidon smoke blots out the sky:
On Tripoli, Benghazi fire shall rain,
And multitudes cremate *before* they die:

VII.20 The eastern empire weakens, totters, falls: [3]
Each satrapy pulls down its former chief.
The new regime the garrisons recalls:
The citizens wake up in disbelief:

VII.20 Ekaterinburg, once again prepare [4]
To see your ruler come to meet his end:
In coldest blood he shall be murdered there
With wife and children, unless heaven forfend:

VII.20 Near Cancer's Tropic, three in Cancer standing, [5]
Mankind shall take another mighty stride
And, leaving Earth behind and cares aside
On quite another planet make a landing:

VII.20 After denials, lies, and long evasion [6]
The mighty chief at last admits defeat;
The first to tender such a resignation
Rather than lawful punishment to meet:

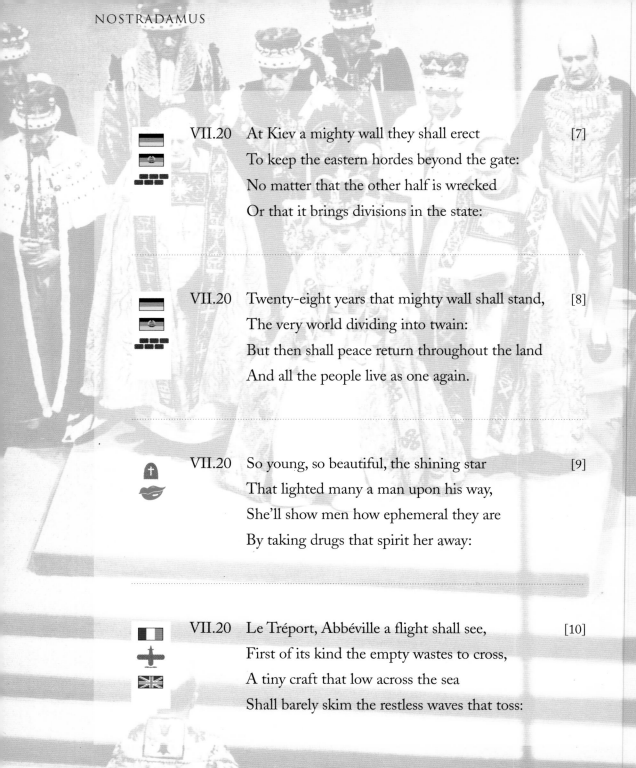

VII.20   At Kiev a mighty wall they shall erect   [7]
To keep the eastern hordes beyond the gate:
No matter that the other half is wrecked
Or that it brings divisions in the state:

VII.20   Twenty-eight years that mighty wall shall stand,   [8]
The very world dividing into twain:
But then shall peace return throughout the land
And all the people live as one again.

VII.20   So young, so beautiful, the shining star   [9]
That lighted many a man upon his way,
She'll show men how ephemeral they are
By taking drugs that spirit her away:

VII.20   Le Tréport, Abbéville a flight shall see,   [10]
First of its kind the empty wastes to cross,
A tiny craft that low across the sea
Shall barely skim the restless waves that toss:

VII.20   Three shall set out upon their mighty quest,   [11]
Leaving the Earth and all their kin behind,
To find another world at their behest,
To warnings deaf, and risks and dangers blind:

VII.20   In London, Aachen shall a mighty coup   [12]
O'erthrow the architect of victory:
Even while wondering what next he'll do,
To his surprise, from power ejected, he:

VII.20   New York, Madrid shall see a mighty crash –   [13]
An airborne craft exploding in mid-air:
Three hundred killed, their bodies turned to ash,
Wreckage o'er land or sea strewn everywhere:

VII.20   Taiyuan, Niigata, mourn your many dead: [14]
A mighty quake shall untold thousands kill.
A million injured, shaking, filled with dread,
Yet others sapped of courage, strength, and will:

VII.20   The mighty continent shall be divided,   [15]

Its two great kingdoms go their separate ways,

Both free at last, their purposes decided,

To plan their destinies in future days:

VII.21   A friend of presidents, beloved by all,

Yet sad, depressed, a victim of her fame,

Into a coma she shall quietly fall,

Bequeathing just her image and her name.

VII.27   A single man that small craft shall control,

By those who meet him seen as strange and odd,

Proud to fulfill his pioneering role

And glad once more to tread the lowly sod.

VII.28   While Earth is quiet, before war starts again,   [1]

In Libra Venus and in Taurus Saturn,

While Jupiter in Virgo still shall reign,

Such is man's quest, and such the planets' pattern.

VII.28 As the Free Leader, sundered from his land,   [2]
Mustering his forces, sails the ocean o'er,
Fomenting trouble with a heavy hand,
Invasion shall provoke a civil war:

VII.28 They'll know there's no retreating from their goal   [3]
Until that far objective they have reached,
No peace for human heart, or mind, or soul
Till on that distant shore their craft has beached.

VII.33 As president, a leader most effective:
Both diplomat and statesman he'll combine,
Yet morally more than a touch defective.
In Washington or Lisbon he'll resign.

VII.35 Sun, Venus, Mercury in Cancer met,
Uranus too, while Jupiter the Bull,
Saturn the Lion rides: do not forget
What shall befall you once the moon is full!

VII.36 He shall not rant or rail against his fate,
But shall retire to let the new powers in.
No matter: blood-lust shall pervade the state,
The world recoil at such a grisly sin.

VII.39 Ride on in triumph through Persepolis,
Yet, hated King, the man in black beware.
Language shall fail, though love bestow a kiss:
Abroad you'll die, and find your gravestone there.

VII.50 Whom freedom saves, it first attempts to drown:
No former slave knows how to swim again.
Three years and seventy are turned upside down –
Yet license shall instead of freedom reign.

VII.55 On terrorists they'll try to place the blame,
Or alien force, or fault mechanical,
Or fire electric: none they'll ever name
Nor satisfy the poor bereaved at all.

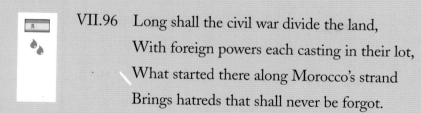

VII.96   Long shall the civil war divide the land,

         With foreign powers each casting in their lot,

         What started there along Morocco's strand

         Brings hatreds that shall never be forgot.

VIII.01   Hooded the moon, bloody the setting sun,

         Skies clouded with the dust, rivers turned red,

         Many shall think the last days have begun:

         Mars in the Archer comes to claim his dead.

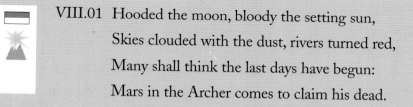

VIII.03   Their city to protect, they shall not fight,

         But cross the river to the other side.

         Their forces quietly steal away at night:

         New powers roll through it in a mighty tide.

VIII.19   In Taurus Saturn, Jupiter, and three   [1]

         In Virgo, fire shall fall from out the sky.

         Mars shoots his bolts, while Neptune rules the sea.

         The city burns, infernal death looms nigh:

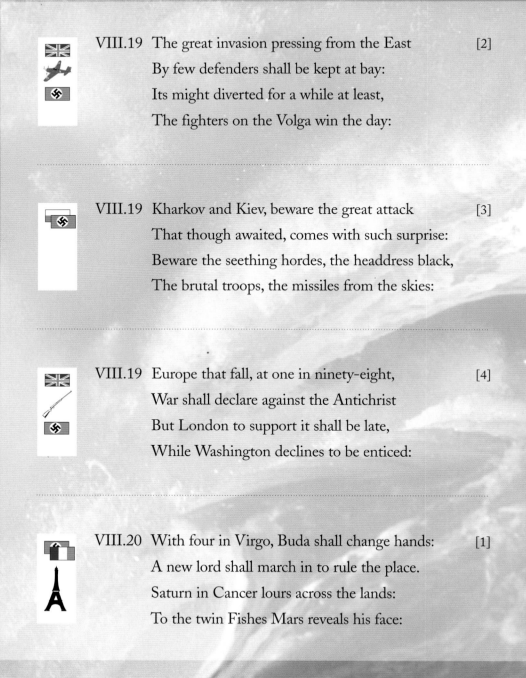

VIII.19   The great invasion pressing from the East   [2]
         By few defenders shall be kept at bay:
         Its might diverted for a while at least,
         The fighters on the Volga win the day:

VIII.19   Kharkov and Kiev, beware the great attack   [3]
         That though awaited, comes with such surprise:
         Beware the seething hordes, the headdress black,
         The brutal troops, the missiles from the skies:

VIII.19   Europe that fall, at one in ninety-eight,   [4]
         War shall declare against the Antichrist
         But London to support it shall be late,
         While Washington declines to be enticed:

VIII.20   With four in Virgo, Buda shall change hands: [1]
         A new lord shall march in to rule the place.
         Saturn in Cancer lours across the lands:
         To the twin Fishes Mars reveals his face:

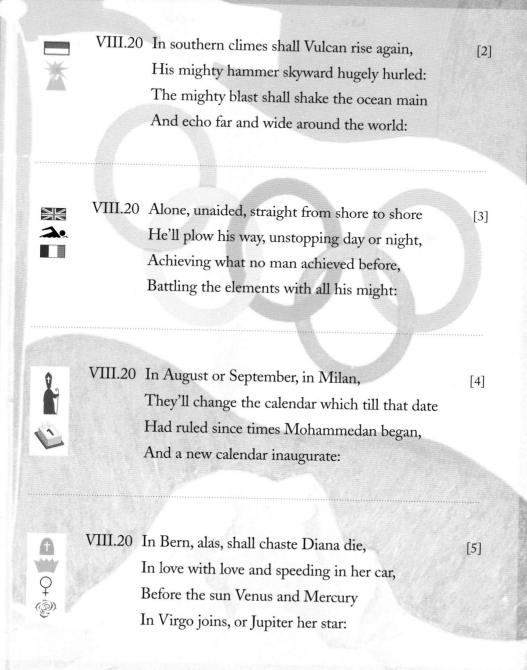

VIII.20   In southern climes shall Vulcan rise again,   [2]
          His mighty hammer skyward hugely hurled:
          The mighty blast shall shake the ocean main
          And echo far and wide around the world:

VIII.20   Alone, unaided, straight from shore to shore   [3]
          He'll plow his way, unstopping day or night,
          Achieving what no man achieved before,
          Battling the elements with all his might:

VIII.20   In August or September, in Milan,   [4]
          They'll change the calendar which till that date
          Had ruled since times Mohammedan began,
          And a new calendar inaugurate:

VIII.20   In Bern, alas, shall chaste Diana die,   [5]
          In love with love and speeding in her car,
          Before the sun Venus and Mercury
          In Virgo joins, or Jupiter her star:

VIII.20 Thus is the coming of the new Messiah: [6]
His birth shall be in Rome or north of it,
Perhaps in northern Spain: the stars require
No less, theirs being unending Holy Writ:

VIII.20 Of Barcelona shall the fair princess – [7]
A brilliant star and ruler of men's hearts –
Fall prey to fate and to her own success
There on the mountains, ere the autumn starts:

VIII.21 Though not the first to reach the further shore,
It is their name posterity shall hold
As founders of the new world evermore
Till planets cease to be and suns grow cold.

VIII.25 Departing for their second, final time,
The doughty founders, all five score and one,
Into their heavy-laden craft shall climb
And start upon their voyage 'neath the sun:

VIII.30 Where once *anno propheti* ruled supreme,
Once more shall *anno domini* prevail,
The solar disk regain its old esteem,
The lunar crescent weaken and then fail.

VIII.38 Sun Virgo exiting – the fact's propitious –
Jupiter, Venus, moon in Leo met:
Such are the stars of that event auspicious,
And such the signs that shall their limits set.

VIII.41 In Libra Saturn and in Leo sun,
Hermes in Virgo, Venus in the Crab,
From Ram to Gemini the moon shall run:
Then death's dread sting her in the heart shall stab.

VIII.52 In Lion sun, in Lion Venus too,
Aquarius Saturn, moon from thence to Fishes,
Then to the dry land of the Bull and Ewe –
There lies his course, and there his watery wishes.

VIII.56 Mighty the shock that such a great princess,
So young, so vital, should depart so soon.
A sea of flowers shall mark a world's distress
When night reclaims the lady of the moon.

VIII.98 In August 'ninety-nine war starts again, [1]
But this time London joins the bloody fray.
In twenty fifty-eight He'll still remain,
Until new powers at last shall win the day.

VIII.98 Yet in his mountain lair the lord shall quake [2]
For all the brutal force of his attack:
Aghast at the decision he must take
'Neath skies of green and yellow, red and black.

VIII.99 Hail to the heroes of the Black Sea shore
Who'll fight to keep so many strong and free!
Hail to the keepers of the eastern door
Who shall so few and yet so doughty be!

IX.06 "The thing cannot be done," they long shall say:
     "Nature, or God, or human flesh forbid it."
     But he shall simply turn and say, "I did it" –
     And lo, all barriers shall melt away.

IX.07 Long years his country shall extol that feat,
     His fame be celebrated, not his failings,
     His victory safe, his name beyond defeat,
     For all his sicknesses at all his sailings.

IX.08 Yet with the years shall power go to his head:
     He'll play the god, and rule that what he thinks
     Is holy writ, standing in scripture's stead,
     Until his empire into turmoil sinks.

IX.20 Faced with the threat of missiles from the sky   [1]
     The Northern powers shall threaten all the Earth
     With war, unless the fortress puts them by
     And sends them back to where they took their birth:

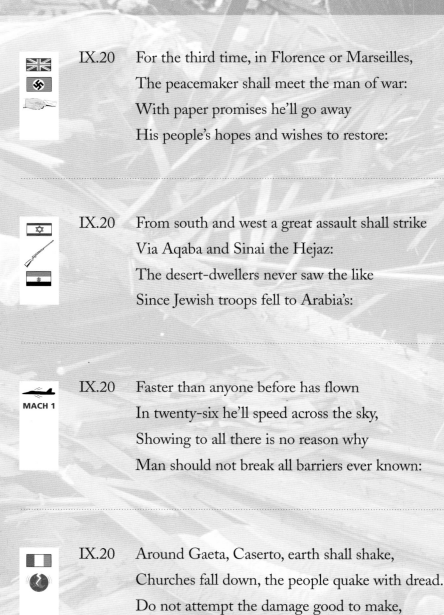

IX.20   For the third time, in Florence or Marseilles,   [2]

The peacemaker shall meet the man of war:

With paper promises he'll go away

His people's hopes and wishes to restore:

IX.20   From south and west a great assault shall strike   [3]

Via Aqaba and Sinai the Hejaz:

The desert-dwellers never saw the like

Since Jewish troops fell to Arabia's:

IX.20   Faster than anyone before has flown   [4]

In twenty-six he'll speed across the sky,

Showing to all there is no reason why

Man should not break all barriers ever known:

IX.20   Around Gaeta, Caserto, earth shall shake,   [5]

Churches fall down, the people quake with dread.

Do not attempt the damage good to make,

Lest more quakes topple walls and strike you dead:

IX.20   At thirty-seven degrees the tireless chief   [6]

Who led the endless march into the west,

At length returned, shall bring his land relief,

And with its riches all his folk invest:

IX.20   Lisbon or Ankara shall see him die,   [7]

The Church's leader of a bare few weeks.

Many, surprised, shall wonder how and why,

And ask why none in power the reason seeks:

IX.20   At Prague, in autumn twenty forty-nine,   [8]

The task of reconciling once begun,

All shall themselves to unity resign:

Once more the land divided shall be one:

IX.21   Awhile the world shall hang on tenterhooks

Until the bluff is called, the threat reduced,

The ships return like starlings, crows, or rooks

At eventide, each to its homely roost.

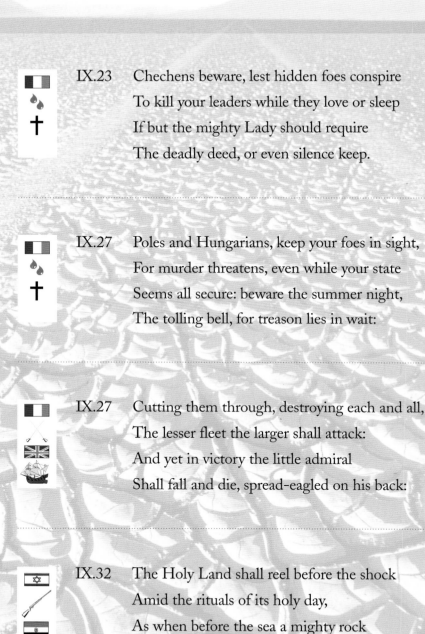

IX.23   Chechens beware, lest hidden foes conspire
To kill your leaders while they love or sleep
If but the mighty Lady should require
The deadly deed, or even silence keep.

IX.27   Poles and Hungarians, keep your foes in sight,   [1]
For murder threatens, even while your state
Seems all secure: beware the summer night,
The tolling bell, for treason lies in wait:

IX.27   Cutting them through, destroying each and all,   [2]
The lesser fleet the larger shall attack:
And yet in victory the little admiral
Shall fall and die, spread-eagled on his back:

IX.32   The Holy Land shall reel before the shock
Amid the rituals of its holy day,
As when before the sea a mighty rock
Shall shudder at the sea's and storm's affray.

IX.37   Is it the heart, as words official claim?

Is it foul poison once administered?

The facts are clear. Corruption he would name,

Scandals expose by those who've greatly erred.

IX.49   The frontiers shall come down, the folk rejoice,

The currencies be merged, the land at one,

The leaders speak with but a single voice,

Fireworks explode, peace reign beneath the sun.

IX.56   Yet he'll achieve no more than a delay,   [1]

His words of peace be omens of disaster.

With Mars in Cancer war's not far away:

For all his efforts, doom draws on the faster.

IX.56   From town to town the quaking earth shall spread, [2]

The people wonder if the end is nigh:

Yet peace shall once again return instead

And all give thanks, and praise the Lord on high.

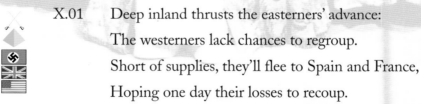

IX.63 Yet in due time the counterblow shall fall:
Suez, Kuwait, or else Wenchow, Ningpo
Two searing strokes from heaven shall undergo
And choke to death beneath an inky pall.

IX.99 Prague, Cracow, Kiev, or Kharkov blitzed with flame –
Fifty degrees shall hold the answer soon.
The children flee, each labeled with a name:
From Crab to Scorpion crawls the darkling moon.

X.01 Deep inland thrusts the easterners' advance:
The westerners lack chances to regroup.
Short of supplies, they'll flee to Spain and France,
Hoping one day their losses to recoup.

X.03 From there he'll sweep from triumph to success,
Success to triumph, till he takes his seat
As emperor whom all alike confess
For bringing them prosperity so sweet.

X.06   The mighty bird shall mount into the sky
Once and once only, bearing him on high
Alone, nor wondering the reason why,
Save to show that his wondrous craft can fly.

X.20   'Twixt forty-six degrees and forty-eight   [1]
With war in stalemate, trials shall begin
Of every captured chief and potentate
For each alleged infraction, crime, or sin:

X.20   The mighty general, turned to ways of peace,   [2]
Shall come to head his country's ruling clique.
This lack of war not everyone shall please:
One of his own to murder him shall seek:

X.20   The desert war that rages to and fro   [3]
Shall be decided when the eastern host
O'ercomes the western with a mighty blow
And hurls them backward all along the coast:

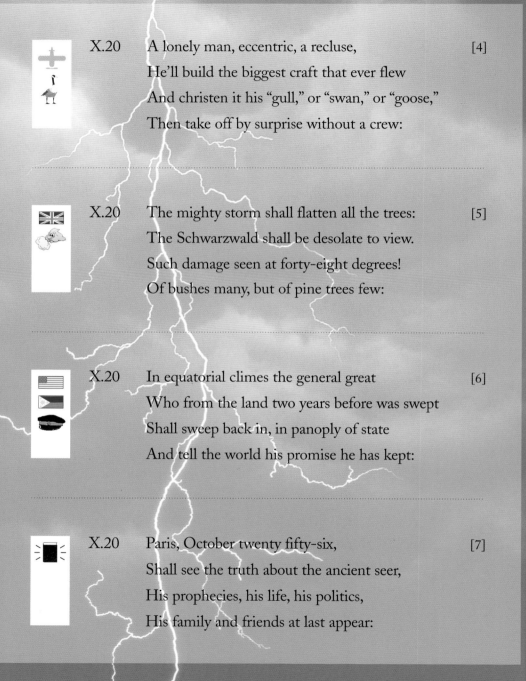

X.20   A lonely man, eccentric, a recluse,   [4]
He'll build the biggest craft that ever flew
And christen it his "gull," or "swan," or "goose,"
Then take off by surprise without a crew:

X.20   The mighty storm shall flatten all the trees: [5]
The Schwarzwald shall be desolate to view.
Such damage seen at forty-eight degrees!
Of bushes many, but of pine trees few:

X.20   In equatorial climes the general great   [6]
Who from the land two years before was swept
Shall sweep back in, in panoply of state
And tell the world his promise he has kept:

X.20   Paris, October twenty fifty-six,   [7]
Shall see the truth about the ancient seer,
His prophecies, his life, his politics,
His family and friends at last appear:

X.20 Near Cairo, 'neath the shifting sands of time [8]

     In twenty-forty shall an ancient tomb

     Or chamber to an ancient paradigm

     Be found again, a precious secret room:

X.20 Near forty-nine degrees, in northeast France, [9]

     A dozen dozen, mainly children, will

     See a whole hillside down on them advance

     And, burying them, their friends and colleagues kill:

X.22 Look to your money, Rome! The time shall come

     When all at once its value shall collapse:

     Your businesses shall hear the final drum,

     Some workers never work again, perhaps:

X.25 Great grief shall sap all France of joy and hope,

     Money be given to fill the parents' lack.

     Alas, no funds can shore up such a slope

     Once it has slid, nor bring the children back.

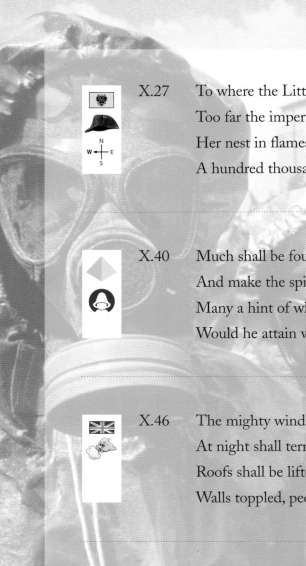

X.27 To where the Little Mother has her seat
Too far the imperious hawk pursues its flight.
Her nest in flames, it beats a sad retreat.
A hundred thousand plumes are turned to white:

X.40 Much shall be found therein to feed the soul
And make the spirit soar; much food for thought;
Many a hint of what must man befall,
Would he attain what he has always sought.

X.46 The mighty wind none shall aright foresee:
At night shall terror spread throughout the land.
Roofs shall be lifted, broken every tree,
Walls toppled, people killed on every hand.

X.56 No longer shall rank superstition reign,
No longer shall disinformation spread:
At last his words shall ring aloud again,
Revealing clearly what was in his head.

X.66 Mighty investments scarce shall rate a penny:
Black Tuesday once again shall rear its head.
Of riches you shall scarcely cling to any
And thank God just to find a crust of bread.

XI.00 Even while chiefs negotiate a peace
The attack shall come. The treachery bodes ill.
Millions shall die before the battle cease.
The greater treachery, the greater will.

XI.04 No matter what the crime or where committed,
No higher officer for it can answer.
Sentence is passed, nor one of them acquitted:
Sun, Venus, Scorpio; Saturn, moon in Cancer.

XI.14 A born inventor, seer of times to come,
His new device shall all the world amaze:
Of ages new he'll beat the herald's drum
And open up the road to future days.

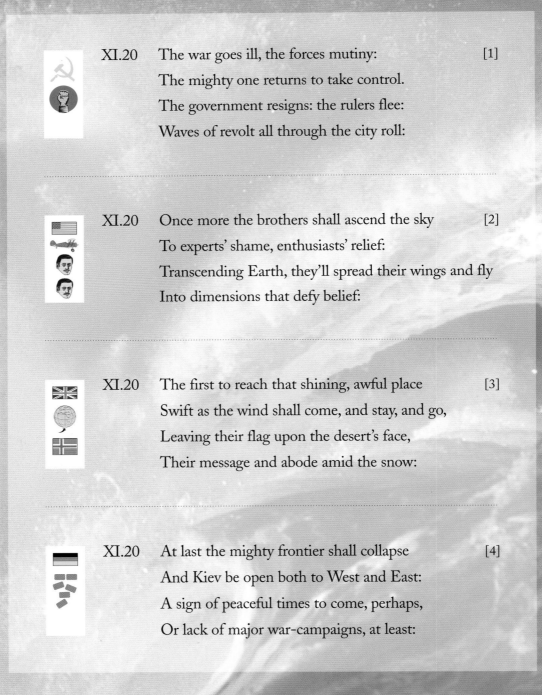

XI.20
The war goes ill, the forces mutiny: [1]
The mighty one returns to take control.
The government resigns: the rulers flee:
Waves of revolt all through the city roll:

XI.20
Once more the brothers shall ascend the sky [2]
To experts' shame, enthusiasts' relief:
Transcending Earth, they'll spread their wings and fly
Into dimensions that defy belief:

XI.20
The first to reach that shining, awful place [3]
Swift as the wind shall come, and stay, and go,
Leaving their flag upon the desert's face,
Their message and abode amid the snow:

XI.20
At last the mighty frontier shall collapse [4]
And Kiev be open both to West and East:
A sign of peaceful times to come, perhaps,
Or lack of major war-campaigns, at least:

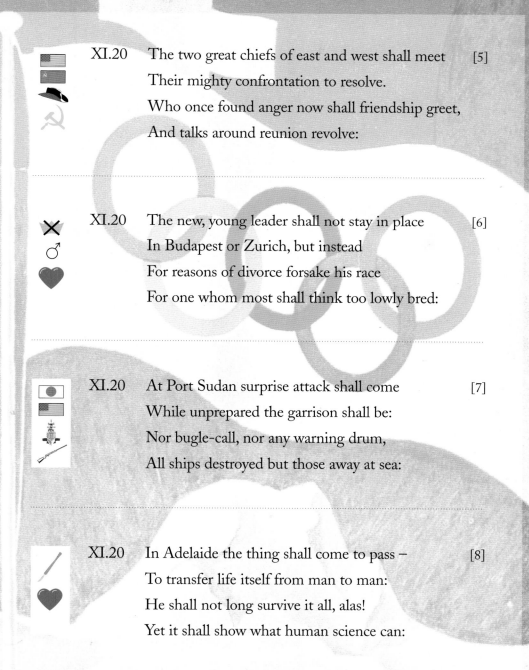

XI.20 The two great chiefs of east and west shall meet [5]
Their mighty confrontation to resolve.
Who once found anger now shall friendship greet,
And talks around reunion revolve:

XI.20 The new, young leader shall not stay in place [6]
In Budapest or Zurich, but instead
For reasons of divorce forsake his race
For one whom most shall think too lowly bred:

XI.20 At Port Sudan surprise attack shall come [7]
While unprepared the garrison shall be:
Nor bugle-call, nor any warning drum,
All ships destroyed but those away at sea:

XI.20 In Adelaide the thing shall come to pass – [8]
To transfer life itself from man to man:
He shall not long survive it all, alas!
Yet it shall show what human science can:

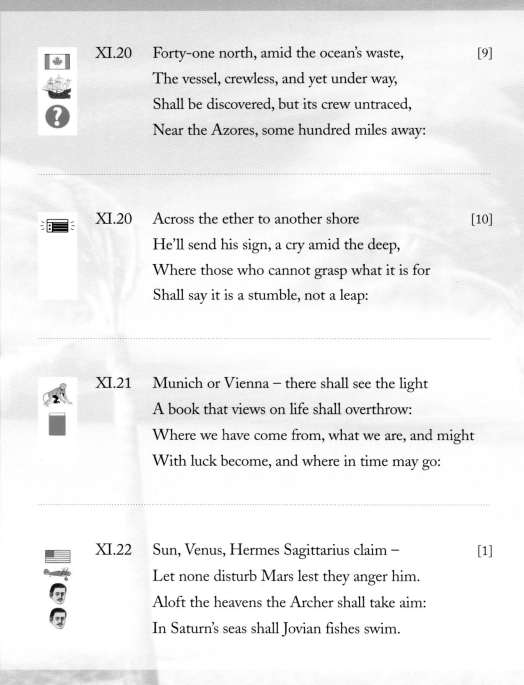

XI.20   Forty-one north, amid the ocean's waste,   [9]

The vessel, crewless, and yet under way,

Shall be discovered, but its crew untraced,

Near the Azores, some hundred miles away:

XI.20   Across the ether to another shore   [10]

He'll send his sign, a cry amid the deep,

Where those who cannot grasp what it is for

Shall say it is a stumble, not a leap:

XI.21   Munich or Vienna – there shall see the light

A book that views on life shall overthrow:

Where we have come from, what we are, and might

With luck become, and where in time may go:

XI.22   Sun, Venus, Hermes Sagittarius claim –   [1]

Let none disturb Mars lest they anger him.

Aloft the heavens the Archer shall take aim:

In Saturn's seas shall Jovian fishes swim.

XI.22 The trace of all that passed the human mind [2]
    Or lived in memory since time began
    Or that all human history has left behind
    Shall be laid bare by that ingenious man:

XI.23 Jupiter rules the Lion; sun, moon the Scales;
    In Virgo Venus, Mars, and Saturn slow.
    What war could not, achieve the winter gales:
    Mars, Venus, Scales; the sun in Scorpio.

XI.25 Long years of war at least shall cease to be:
    The powers shall settle on an armistice.
    Upon a time and hour they shall agree,
    The slaughter stop, the bells ring out for peace:

XI.26 The little genius playing out his heart [1]
    Entrances all, packing the concert room:
    Yet all too young he shall play out his part
    And, scarce-lamented, find a pauper's tomb:

XI.26   In Scorpio sun and Mercury, in Lion   [2]
Both Jupiter and Saturn: thus the signs
That doctors of the time can sure rely on
When human life with life henceforth combines.

XI.35   The cannon sounds: the Scottish port is shaken.
The navy mutinies: the deed is done.
New powers restore the liberties once taken.
Freedom's new slavery has just begun.

XI.44   A new world order then shall grow apace,
The west grow strong, the east grow weak and die.
For man new visions shall the old replace.
A comet shall traverse the darkling sky.

XI.48   In Scorpio sun, and moon, and Mercury,
In Sagittarius Venus, Jove in Cancer:
Saturn in tricky Capricorn, where he
Shall rule a truce, if not the final answer.

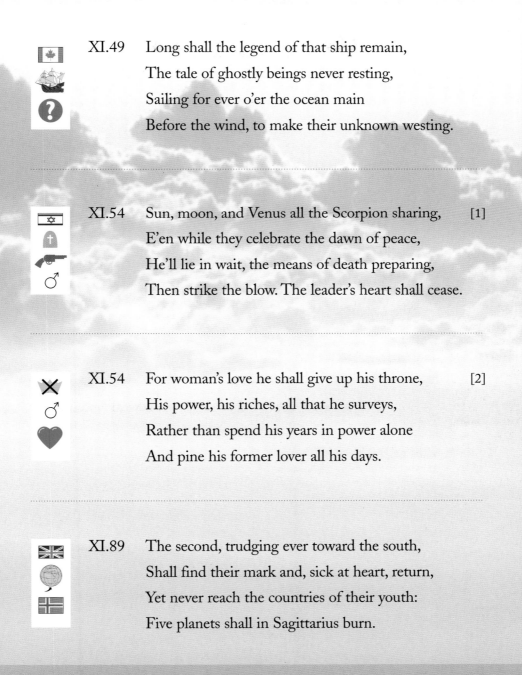

XI.49 Long shall the legend of that ship remain,
The tale of ghostly beings never resting,
Sailing for ever o'er the ocean main
Before the wind, to make their unknown westing.

XI.54 Sun, moon, and Venus all the Scorpion sharing, [1]
E'en while they celebrate the dawn of peace,
He'll lie in wait, the means of death preparing,
Then strike the blow. The leader's heart shall cease.

XI.54 For woman's love he shall give up his throne, [2]
His power, his riches, all that he surveys,
Rather than spend his years in power alone
And pine his former lover all his days.

XI.89 The second, trudging ever toward the south,
Shall find their mark and, sick at heart, return,
Yet never reach the countries of their youth:
Five planets shall in Sagittarius burn.

XI.92   His sun and Mercury the Scorpion stings,
                His Jupiter rules over Virgin youth:
                His Saturn wavers as his song he sings
                And suffocates the symphonies of Truth.

XI.94   Where Paris leads, the world at large shall follow,
                Heroes return to lands that them befit,
                The bells ring loud as shall the claim ring hollow:
                The triple Scorpion shall vouch for it.

XI.97   Many shall say it contradicts the lore
                That heretofore has guided man aright:
                Others shall say it pierces to the core
                Of humanness, and points us toward the light.

XII.08   Of revolution he shall be the voice,
                Of faith and all that's noblest in mankind:
                In brotherhood and freedom he'll rejoice,
                Yet to his own song deaf, and suffering blind.

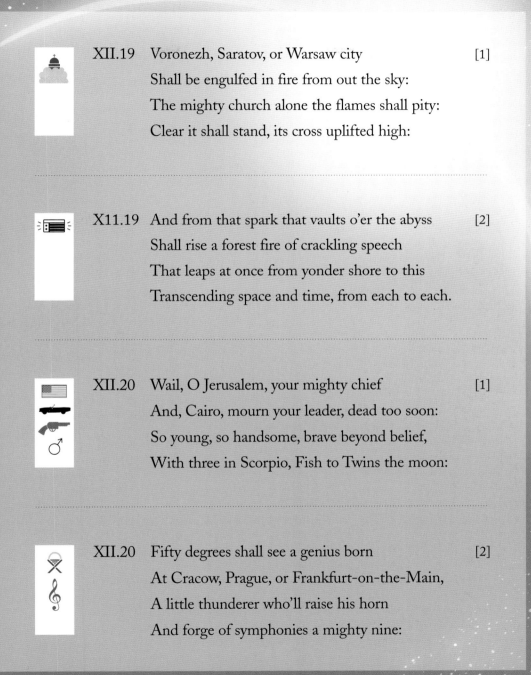

XII.19   Voronezh, Saratov, or Warsaw city   [1]

Shall be engulfed in fire from out the sky:

The mighty church alone the flames shall pity:

Clear it shall stand, its cross uplifted high:

X11.19   And from that spark that vaults o'er the abyss   [2]

Shall rise a forest fire of crackling speech

That leaps at once from yonder shore to this

Transcending space and time, from each to each.

XII.20   Wail, O Jerusalem, your mighty chief   [1]

And, Cairo, mourn your leader, dead too soon:

So young, so handsome, brave beyond belief,

With three in Scorpio, Fish to Twins the moon:

XII.20   Fifty degrees shall see a genius born   [2]

At Cracow, Prague, or Frankfurt-on-the-Main,

A little thunderer who'll raise his horn

And forge of symphonies a mighty nine:

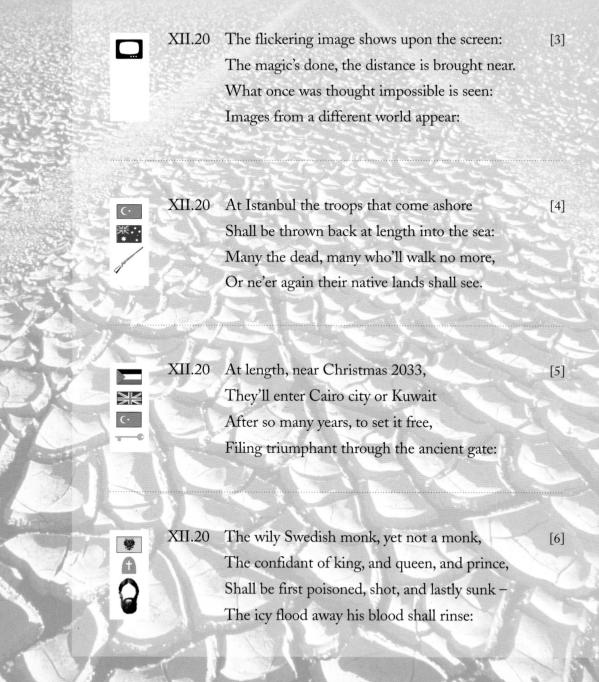

XII.20 The flickering image shows upon the screen: [3]
The magic's done, the distance is brought near.
What once was thought impossible is seen:
Images from a different world appear:

XII.20 At Istanbul the troops that come ashore [4]
Shall be thrown back at length into the sea:
Many the dead, many who'll walk no more,
Or ne'er again their native lands shall see.

XII.20 At length, near Christmas 2033, [5]
They'll enter Cairo city or Kuwait
After so many years, to set it free,
Filing triumphant through the ancient gate:

XII.20 The wily Swedish monk, yet not a monk, [6]
The confidant of king, and queen, and prince,
Shall be first poisoned, shot, and lastly sunk –
The icy flood away his blood shall rinse:

XII.20   In Edinburgh the old flag shall come down,   [7]
          A new be raised, the former ruler fall,
          The shades of empire quit the ancient town
          Which "nation's capital" they'll gladly call:

XII.20   The noble prisoner, so long confined   [8]
          In the far south shall leave his prison cell.
          Twenty-six years no bitterness shall find:
          Out he shall walk, triumphant, old, yet well:

XII.20   In Tunis or Algiers the die is cast: [9]
          Suddenly from the sky a mighty priest,
          Black-clad and bearded, from the ancient past
          Shall pounce on you like some ferocious beast:

XII.22   So loved, applauded, riding in his car
          Triumphant down the highway to the city:
          One from above shall kill him from afar,
          And others maim. O woe! O shock! O pity!

XII.26   Flee, flee, great king! Your final hour is nigh!

Your people shall rejoice at your demise.

Th' old order falls, its time of glory by,

As the black priest descends from out the skies.

XII.33   From halfway round the world their flags shall come

But then, repulsed, to other fronts deployed,

Renew the fight the Muslims to o'ercome

Until at length their empire is destroyed.

XII.34   A peasant healer, holy man, and seer,

He'll rise to power by influence personal:

But in the end too powerful appear,

Too dangerous, in fact, to live at all.

XII.35   Four times the foe to throw them out shall try,

But now the tide of freedom shall prevail:

The tribes and western forces shall ally,

The mighty Muslim dispensation fail.

XII.43   Sun, Jupiter in Capricorn residing,

Mercury's gift in Sagittarius

Is speech transcendent, every truth confiding,

Nor in that revelation aught nefarious.

XII.48   Ere long he'll be the leader of his people,

Freedom proclaimed for master and for slave:

Joy shall ring out from every church and steeple,

Race live with race, justice reward the brave.

XII.50   Great the rejoicing at fair freedom's dawning;

Great the excitement at the risks to come:

Yet some there'll be who'll turn instead to mourning

For ancient certainties 'neath Britain's thumb.

XII.99   In Sagittarius sun and Mercury;

In Ram, Bull, Twins the moon; Saturn in Taurus;

In Scorpio Venus – thus the signs shall be,

Just as they once before stood clearly o'er us.

BIBLIOGRAPHY

*European/American publishers are indicated
by slash-marks*

1   ALLEMAND, J. Nostradamus et les hiéroglyphes
    (Maison de Nostradamus, Salon, 1996/)

2   AMADOU, R. L'Astrologie de Nostradamus
    (ARRC, Poissy, 1992/)

3   BECKLEY (ed.) Nostradamus's Unpublished
    Prophecies *(Inner Light, 1991)*

4   BENAZRA, R. Répertoire Chronologique
    Nostradamique (1545-1989) *(1990)*

5   BOESER, K. (ed.) The Elixirs of Nostradamus
    (Bloomsbury/HarperCollins, 1995)

6   BOESER, K. Nostradamus *(Bloomsbury, 1994/)*

7   BRENNAN, J.H. Nostradamus; Visions of the
    Future *(Aquarian, 1992/)*

8   BRIND'AMOUR, P. Nostradamus astrophile
    (/University of Ottawa, 1993)

9   BRIND'AMOUR, P. Nostradamus: Les premières
    centuries ou prophéties *(Droz, 1996/)*

10 CANNON, D. Conversations with Nostradamus:
    His Prophecies Explained, 3 vols.
    (/Ozark Mountain, 1989 onward)

11 CAPEL, S. Nostradamus: His Life and
    Predictions *(Studio Editions, 1995/)*

12 CHEETHAM, E. The Final Prophecies of
    Nostradamus *(Futura/Perigree, 1989)*

13 CHEETHAM, E. The Further Prophecies of
    Nostradamus *(Corgi/Perigree, 1985-91)*

14 CHEETHAM, E. The Prophecies of Nostradamus
    (Corgi/Perigree, 1973 /Berkley, 1981)

15 CHOMARAT, M., DUPÈBE, J. & POLIZZI, G.
    Nostradamus ou le savoir transmis
    (Chomarat, 1997/)

16 CHOMARAT, M. & LAROCHE, DR. J.-P.
    Bibliographie Nostradamus *(Koerner, 1989/)*

17 DUFRESNE, M. Nostradamus: Première
    Centurie (series) up to Nostradamus: Septième
    Centurie, 7 vols. *(/Chicoutimi/JCL, 1989-97)*

18 DUPÈBE, J. Nostradamus – Lettres Inédites
    (Droz, 1983/)

19 ERICKSTAD, H.G.B. The Prophecies of
    Nostradamus in Historical Order
    (Janus, 1996/Vantage, 1982)

20 FONTBRUNE, J.-C. DE Nostradamus 1:
    Countdown to Apocalypse
    (Pan/Holt, 1983; Cresset, 1993, Pt. 1)

21 FONTBRUNE, J.-C. DE Nostradamus 2:
    Into the Twenty-First Century
    (/Holt, 1984; Cresset, 1993, Pt. 2)

22 HAPGOOD, C.H. Maps of the Ancient
    Sea-Kings *(Turnstone, 1979/)*

23 HEWITT, V.J. Nostradamus: The Key to the
    Centuries *(Hutchinson, 1994/)*

24 HEWITT, V.J. & LORIE, P. Nostradamus:
    the End of the Millennium
    (Bloomsbury/Simon & Schuster, 1991)

25 HOGUE, J. Nostradamus and the Millennium *(Bloomsbury, 1987/)*

26 HOGUE, J. Nostradamus: The Complete Prophecies *(Element/Element, 1997)*

27 HOGUE, J. Nostradamus: The New Revelations *(Element/Element, 1994)*

28 IONESCU, V. Les dernières victoires de Nostradamus *(Filipacchi, 1993/)*

29 KIDOGO, BARDO *(Barry Popkess)* The Keys to the Predictions of Nostradamus *(Foulsham, 1994/)*

30 KING, FRANCIS X. Nostradamus: Prophecies Fulfilled and Predictions for the Millennium and Beyond *(BCA, 1993/)*

31 LAVER, J. Nostradamus or the Future Foretold *(Mann, 1942-81/)*

32 LEMESURIER, P. The Nostradamus Encyclopedia *(Godsfield/St Martin's, 1997)*

33 LEMESURIER, P. Nostradamus: The Final Reckoning *(Piatkus, 1995/Berkley, 1997)*

34 LEMESURIER, P. Nostradamus – The Next 50 Years *(Piatkus, 1993/Berkley, 1994)*

35 LEONI, E. Nostradamus and His Prophecies *(/Wings, 1961-82)*

36 LEROY, DR. E. Nostradamus: ses origines, sa vie, son oeuvre *(Lafitte, 1993/)*

37 LORIE, P. *(with Greene, L.)* Nostradamus: The Millennium and Beyond *(Bloomsbury/Simon & Schuster, 1993)*

38 LORIE, P. *(with Mascetti)* Nostradamus's Prophecies for Women *(Bloomsbury, 1995/)*

39 DE MAREUIL, J. Les ultimes prophéties de Nostradamus *(Grancher, 1994/)*

40 MÉZO, E. Ainsi parlait Nostradamus *(du Rocher, 1995-6/)*

41 NOSTRADAMUS, M. Lettre à Catherine de Médicis *(Chomarat, 1996/)*

42 NOSTRADAMUS, M. Orus Apollo *(ed. Rollet, P. as* Interprétation des hiéroglyphes de Horapollo) *(Marcel Petit, 1993/)*

43 NOSTRADAMUS, M. Les Prophéties, Lyon 1557 *(Chomarat, 1993/)*

44 NOSTRADAMUS, M. Traité des fardemens et des confitures *(published as* Le Vray et Parfait Embellissement de la Face *in Plantin's Antwerp edition of 1557)* *(Gutenberg Reprints, 1979/)*

45 OVASON, D. The Secrets of Nostradamus *(Century, 1997/)*

46 PITT FRANCIS, D. Nostradamus: Prophecies of Present Times? *(Aquarian, 1984/)*

47 RANDI, J. The Mask of Nostradamus *(/Prometheus, 1993)*

48 ROBERTS, H.C. The Complete Prophecies of Nostradamus *(Grafton/Nostradamus Co., 1985)*

49 WARD, C.A. Oracles of Nostradamus *(Society of Metaphysicians [facsimile of 1891 ed.] 1990, 1995 /Modern Library [Scribner] 1940)*

50 WOLDBEN, A. *(trans. from Italian)* After 0Nostradamus *(Mayflower/1975)*

INDEX

A

Aachen, 91
Abbéville, 90
Adelaide, 113
Aden, 73
Aix-en-Provence, 12
Alderney, 65
Alexander the Great, 24, 86
Algiers, 121
Almanachs, 12, 14, 17, 21, 41
Amadou, R., 6
Ankara, 70, 103
Antichrist, 26, 45, 52, 96
Apianus, P., 21
Aqaba, 102
Arles, 17
Armenia, 42
Augustus, 23, 24, 25
Avignon, 11, 42, 50, 79, 81
Azores, 114

B

Babylon, 18, 77
Balearics, 50
Balkans, 50
Barcelona, 98
Belgium, 52
Belgrade, 70
Benazra, R., 6
Benghazi, 88
Berlin, 63
Bern, 97
Bibliothèque Nationale, 13
Black Sea, 100
Bordeaux, 12
Bosphorus, 42
Branchidai, 31, 33
Brazzaville, 63
Breda, 26, 28
Brind'Amour, P., 6
Britain, 6, 42, 52, 77, 84, 123
Britanny, 84
British Museum, 13
Bucharest, 70
Buda, 96
Budapest, 113

C

Cairo, 109, 119, 120
Calendar, 48, 97
Carcassonne, 12
Caserto, 102
Catholics, 14
Cecil, W., 14
Centuries, 14–15, 31, 41
Champollion, – 13
Charles IX, 17
Chavigny, J.A. de, 22
Chechens, 104
Chicago, 73
Chomarat, M., 6
Church liturgy, 39, 46
Chyren, 24, 26, 52
Clavicula Salomonis, 31
Colbert, J.B., 13
Colophon, 31
Comparative horoscopy, 7, 30, 34, 39–40, 46, 52, 56
Computerized programs, 23, 29, 34
Copernicus, N., 21
Cracow, 85, 106, 119
Crusaders, 19

D

Danube, 43
Dating code, 23, 29, 38–43, 57
De Launay, - 87
De Mysteriis Aegyptiorum, 31
Declination of Sun, 20
Delphi, 31, 33
D'Encausse, H., 12
Denmark, 52
Diana, 97
Didymi, 31
Dieppe, 78
Dublin, 63
Dufresne, M., 6
Dupèbe, J., 6

E

Edinburgh, 121
Egypt, 42, 46, 50, 62
Ekaterinberg, 89
Elizabeth I, 14, 17

Elohim, 67
England, 14, 17
English Channel, 52
Europe, 17, 23, 35, 42–3, 46, 50, 77, 79, 96
European Union, 46

F

Florence, 21, 102
Four Horsemen of the Apocalypse, 52
France, 6, 12, 14, 19, 24–6, 42–3, 50, 52, 84, 106, 109
François I, 19
Frankfurt, 85, 119
French Revolution, 21

G

Gaeto, 102
Galen, 13
Garancières, – 6
Garonne, 50
Gaugamela, 86
Geneva, 63
Germany, 15, 46
Gerona, 27, 28
Gibraltar, 42, 50
Glanum, 11
Great Conjunction, 7, 19

H

Hejaz, 102
Henri II, 14–5, 17, 34, 39
Henri IV, 17
Henri V, 24–6, 52
Hercules, 52
Hindenburg, 35, 36
Holland, 26, 77
Holy Land, 104
Horographs, 24, 25, 27–8
Hungarians, 104
Hussein, S., 26, 27

I

Iamblichus, 31
Incubation, 32, 59
Inquisition of Toulouse, 12
Iraq, 42

Islam *see also* Muslims, 81
Istanbul, 71, 120
Italy, 19, 42, 50, 52
Izmir, 42

J
Janus, 22
Jerusalem, 119
Jews, 10, 102

K
Kharkov, 78, 85, 96, 106
Kiev, 78, 90, 96, 106, 112
Kinshasa, 63
Kohl, H., 46
Kuwait, 106, 120

L
Laden, O. Bin, 46
Language, 33
Laroche, J.-P., 6
Last Judgment, 52
Le Tréport, 90
Leroy, E., 6
Lisbon, 27, 93, 103
Liturgical datings, 39, 46
Loire, 50
London, 79, 91, 96, 100
Louis XIV, 13
Lyon, 12, 31

M
Mabus, 26–8, 42
Madrid, 24–5, 91
Managua, 73
Marseille, 12, 14, 102
Maubeuge, 26
Médicis, C. de, 15
Mediterranean, 52
Memphis, 80
Messiah, 98
Methodology, 7, 18–21
Michelangelo, 26
Middle East, 19, 35, 50, 52
Milan, 97
Millennium bug, 48
Mirrors, 34
Montpellier, 11
Morocco, 42, 50, 95
Munich, 114
Muslims, 17, 19, 27–8, 42–3, 46, 50–3, 97, 12

N
Naples, 24–5
New Jersey, 35
New Millennium, 44–53
New Prophecies, 7, 54–123
New York, 35, 91
Niigata, 91
Ningpo, 106
Normandy, 78
North Africa, 35, 43, 46, 50
Nostredame, J. de, 10

O
Ogmion, 52
Orus Apollo, 13

P
Paired verses, 40
Paris, 13, 15, 46, 52, 108
Pavia, 19
Periodicities, 34
Persepolis, 94
Plague, 11, 19, 43
Planetary line-ups, 7, 18-22, 48
Poles, 104
Ponsarde, A., 12
Pope, 42–3, 46–7, 50
Port Sudan, 113
Portugal, 27
Prague, 85, 103, 106, 119
Predictions, 42–3, 50–1
Prologue, 57, 58–9
Prophéties, 14–15, 21, 32, 39, 46
Protestants, 14
Pyrenees, 50

R
Rabelais, F., 11
Randi, J., 6
Refugees, 46
Rhône, 50
Rome, 23, 47, 52, 71, 73, 98, 109
Rosetta Stone, 13
Roussat, R., 21

S
St.-Malo, 84
St.-Rémy, J. de, 11
St.-Rémy-de-Provence, 10
Saladin, 19
Salamis, 42
Salon-de-Provence, 12, 15, 17
Sarajevo, 42, 46, 47, 70, 79, 86

Saratov, 119
Saudi Arabia, 26
Scaliger, J.C., 12
Schwarzwald, 108
Scotland, 116
Scrying, 33
Second World War, 23
Serre, L., 12
Sicily, 42
Sidon, 88
Sinai, 102
Spain, 26–8, 42–3, 50, 98, 106
Stadius, J., 13
Suetonius, 24
Suez, 106

T
Taiyun, 91
Tehran, 80
Tests, 34–6
Theurgy, 31, 34, 44
Tripoli, 88
Tunis, 121
Turkey, 31, 42, 46
Turrel, P., 21
TWA flight 800, 35, 36–7
Tyre, 88

U
United States, 26, 52

V
Van Gogh, V., 11
Vesuvius, 43
Vienna, 27, 114
Vinci, L. da, 26
Volga, 72, 79, 96
Voronezh, 119

W
Wales, 73
Warsaw, 119
Washington, 93, 96
Wenchow, 106
Wicklow, 73

Y
Yaroslav, 81

Z
Zürich, 113

ACKNOWLEDGMENTS

Picture Credits

The Publisher wishes to thank the following for use of pictures

Archiv für Kunst und Geschichte, London

Bilbliothèque Municipale de Lyon/Michel Chamouat

The Bridgeman Art Library/Giraudon: Musée Carnavalet, Paris; the Louvre, Paris; and Pinoteca Dei Concordi, Rivigo

Cameron Collection

Peter Lemesurier

Musée de Salon et de la Crau/Musée de Nostradamus, Salon

NASA

Rex Features, London

The Stock Market, London

By the same author:

The Armageddon Script

Beyond All Belief

The Cosmic Eye

Gospel of the Stars

The Great Pyramid Decoded

The Great Pyramid: Your Personal Guide

The Healing of the Gods

This New Age Business

Nostradamus: The Next 50 Years

Nostradamus: The Final Reckoning

The Nostradamus Encyclopedia

Gods of the Dawn

The Essential Nostradamus

Translations:

Through Music to the Self *(Hamel)*

Zen in the Art of the Tea Ceremony *(Hammitzsch)*

The Healing Power of Illness *(Dethlefsen & Dahlke)*

Harmony is the Healer *(von Rohr)*

and see:

Nostradamus: The Next 50 Years

Nostradamus: The Final Reckoning